The Walter Lynwood Fleming
Lectures in Southern History

Louisiana State University

The Legacy of Andrew Jackson

The Legacy of
ANDREW JACKSON

Essays on Democracy,
Indian Removal,
and Slavery

ROBERT V. REMINI

Louisiana State University Press
Baton Rouge

Designer: Albert Crochet
Typeface: Trump Mediaeval
Typesetter: Focus Graphics, Inc.

Library of Congress Cataloging-in-Publication Data

Remini, Robert Vincent, 1921–
    The legacy of Andrew Jackson: essays on democracy, Indian
removal and slavery / Robert V. Remini.
        p.   cm. — (The Walter Lynwood Fleming lectures in southern
history)
        Includes index.
        ISBN 0-8071-1407-3 (cloth)   ISBN 0-8071-1642-4 (paper)
        1. Jackson, Andrew, 1767–1845.   2. United States — Politics and
government — 1829–1837.   3. Indians of North America — Removal.
4. Slavery — United States.   I. Title.   II. Series.
E382.R45 1988
973.5'6 — dc19

The paper in this book meets the guidelines for permanence and
durability of the Committee on Production Guidelines for Book
Longevity of the Council on Library Resources. ∞

Louisiana Paperback Edition, 1990
07 06 05 04 03   10 9 8

For my grandson
Brian Richard Costello

Contents

Acknowledgments

I think it is incumbent upon me at this time to acknowledge the extraordinary amount of support I have received over the years from the University of Illinois. When I first arrived on campus over twenty years ago, the Research Board made it possible for me to purchase microfilm copies of the manuscript papers of Andrew Jackson housed in the Library of Congress. Those microfilms were used not only to advance my own biography of Jackson, then in progress, but microflow copies were made from them that became the initial holdings of the Jackson Papers Project at the Hermitage in Tennessee. The project now possesses copies of over sixty thousand Jackson documents, of which it has already published two volumes in a letterpress edition.

The University of Illinois also made possible research trips to France and England and, by designating me a research professor of humanities, provided me with sufficient time each year to complete a number of writing assignments on Jackson's life and times. Most recently its foundation has named me a University Scholar and awarded me additional funds to pursue further research in the Jacksonian era. No university could have been more supportive in providing time and research funds to encourage scholarship among its faculty. I am profoundly grateful to those responsible, most particularly its higher administration both in Chicago and Urbana.

I also owe a deep debt of gratitude to the Ladies' Hermitage Association for large and small favors over the years, including support for research trips throughout the United States and in Spain. In agreeing to sponsor the Jackson Papers Project, the association recognized in a public way its responsibility to Jackson's name and reputation as a statesman, not simply to the physical remains of his house and its furnishings.

Harriet C. Owsley, the wife of Frank L. Owsley, the distinguished southern historian, served as the first director of the Jackson Project and as an editor of the first volume of the Jackson Papers. She is a very special lady to whom I owe a very special debt because of her unflagging encouragement and assistance over a period of twenty-five years or more. Since I first met her in the manuscript room of the Tennessee Historical Library, she has assisted me in countless ways to find, decipher, transcribe, and edit Jackson manuscripts. She has read drafts of several of my books and offered criticisms and advice based on her long experience and expert knowledge of Tennessee history. She assisted her late husband in his research and writing, and I know from my own personal experience how much she must have contributed to the excellence of his distinguished monographs.

I also extend my thanks to John Easterly, who edited the manuscript and gently prodded me away from colloquialisms, overuse of the passive voice, and many awkward constructions. Finally, I wish to thank once more Professor John Loos and his colleagues at Louisiana State University for the enormous honor of giving the Fleming Lectures and for their hospitality and many courtesies. And would you believe, John Loos is a Yankee!

The Legacy of Andrew Jackson

Preface

I don't think I shall ever forget the day during the annual meeting of the Southern Historical Association when Professor John Loos, chairman of the Department of History at Louisiana State University, stepped up to me, identified himself, and quietly informed me that the members of his department had voted to invite me to present the Walter Lynwood Fleming Lectures at LSU in 1984. I think I looked at him with amazement. I have always regarded the Fleming Lectures as the most prestigious in American history, and I was literally overwhelmed by his invitation. Without a moment's hesitation—without even thinking about a possible topic—I accepted. Then, slowly, after several hours of euphoria, the obligation of my acceptance dawned on me. I had to give three lectures on some aspect of southern history, presumably something I had investigated or was in the process of investigating, something scholarly, something important, and supposedly something on which I could speak with authority. It was at that instant that I began to have second thoughts. What would be the subject of my lectures? It so happened that at the moment I was completing the last book of my three-volume biography of Andrew Jackson. Obviously, Old Hickory was a likely topic, and, I dare say, the faculty at LSU undoubtedly expected me to speak on Jackson or his era but had left the final choice to me. Still, what could I add to what I had already written on Jackson? A repeat of previous material—even with a different slant or "additional facts"—hardly seemed appropriate. No, if Jackson was to be my subject, then I had to offer something different, something special.

I was limited in my preparation by the fact that there were three separate lectures, each to be an entity in itself and each to run approximately fifty minutes. Moreover, each of the three topics, of necessity, had to be important in itself. What I finally decided to undertake was an assessment of Jackson's role and contribution to the questions of democracy, Indian removal, and slavery, and the whole would be entitled "The Jackson Legacy." At the time, I recognized that *legacy* was not precisely the correct word to describe what I was about. It was really not my intention to sum up all the works of Andrew Jackson, both good and bad, that he had bequeathed to posterity. If that had indeed been my intention, I would surely have discussed a number of other things, in particular his contribution in developing the notion that Americans were citizens of an indissoluble Union, that they belonged to a Union of people, not a collection of states. His view, along with its underpinning of constitutional law, provided the basic argument that Lincoln would use in 1861 to deny the southern states the right to secede.

Furthermore, any evaluation of Jackson's contribution to American political history would surely emphasize his role in the final establishment of the modern two-party system. Without his name and reputation it is hard to imagine such men as Martin Van Buren, John C. Calhoun, and others constructing the Democratic party and winning converts from all sections of the country to its particular philosophy. Jackson was essential to the reemergence of the party system following the so-called "Era of Good Feelings." And he took an active part not only in the organizational development of his party but in shaping its ideological content as well.

In addition, Jackson's powerful impact on the presidency would require examination. He strengthened the presidential office to the point that some historians mark the inauguration of the "imperial presidency" at the commencement of his administration. There can be no doubt that he utilized the veto power in a new and creative manner to provide the president with legislative as well as executive authority. He conceived of the president as the tribune of all the people, elected by them and responsible to them. He presumed to argue that the president is the head of the government, the person who sets the nation's priorities and directs its course of action.

Jackson's "war" against the Second Bank of the United States would also invite attention. If nothing else, that war placed a distinctive emphasis on laissez-faire economic policies in the

United States, which—for better or worse—shaped economic development and thinking in this country for over a century. Clearly, then, a series of lectures on Jackson's legacy—and I forbear outlining some of the less attractive features of his legacy—could not be all-embracing, not without requiring many more hours than were available. What I finally decided to do, and what had been in the back of my mind almost from the moment I gave the lectures serious thought, was to select three subjects that were especially significant and about which there was controversy, misunderstanding, or lack of appreciation, and on which I felt I had more of substance to say. Using these criteria, I automatically excluded the Bank War. I have written a small book on it and further elaborated on the subject in my subsequent biography. I have said enough about the matter and have nothing more to add. Similarly, I decided against a further statement concerning the Nullification Controversy and Jackson's role in it. No one seriously doubts Jackson's extraordinary devotion to the Union or his determination to preserve it at all costs. At one point not long ago I think Jackson's important contribution to the debate over the nature of the Union lacked adequate appreciation among historians. But the publication of Kenneth M. Stampp's magnificent study *The Imperiled Union: Essays on the Background of the Civil War* (New York, 1980) dramatically altered that situation. Stampp's essay clearly delineates Jackson's towering importance to the evolution of modern thinking about the nature of the Union. Whatever additional statements I had to make on the subject were included in my biography.

My choices for the three lectures, therefore, devolved upon the questions of democracy, Indian removal, and slavery. When it comes right down to it, I regard Jackson's contribution to the development of democracy in this country as his greatest contribution. And although I had discussed this question at length in the biography, I felt I had more to say, particularly in emphasizing his advanced thinking about the direct election of governmental officeholders. Besides, I do not find that he is given sufficient credit for his role in that development. Frankly, I don't think there are many historians who are aware of Jackson's extraordinarily liberal views on the suffrage. They do not appreciate his deep commitment to the notion of majority rule. By and large, their understanding of his ideas about government begins and ends with his commitment to the federal structure, states' rights, and a severely limited central government. Far more fundamental, I think, is his even stronger view that "the majority is to rule." Also, I felt that much more needed to be said about his attitude toward the judiciary—his horror of their elitist inclinations and their presumption about interpreting the Constitution as a final authority. Unfortunately, he did not expound his ideas in any formal and systematic way, and they must be culled from interviews he had with such reporters as Frank Blair and George Bancroft. And although Jackson by his words and actions throughout his administration quickened the nation's demand for greater democracy, he was too far ahead of his own generation—and maybe too far ahead of any American generation—to succeed in altering the basic republican structure of government. In that sense Jackson was out of step with his generation. He advocated more than they were prepared to handle, probably more than most Americans today are willing to accept. As a result, the manner in which presidents and members of Congress are elected, the doctrine of judicial review, and the appointment of federal judges for life—all survived the phenomenon we call Jacksonian Democracy. Thus, because Jackson's important and advanced views regarding democracy have not been generally known or appreciated, and because of his significant contribution to the advance of democracy in America, despite the failure to advance it as far as he had hoped, I decided that this topic must constitute the basis for my first lecture.

For the subject of the second lecture I quickly decided on the removal of the Indians, and this decision was based on a number of considerations. To begin with, it is the one topic today that invites the sharpest criticism of Jackson. He is condemned virtually out of hand for the horrors of that event. Few historians, I find, are willing to grant any other motive for removal than greed, psychological trauma, political opportunism, or some other base intention. To suggest that Jackson might have had nobler feelings toward the Indian is to invite ridicule. And to argue that removal might have been prompted by a wide mix of reasons and emotions, like most human behavior, is hardly tolerated, even by those who should know better. The fact that the adoption of the policy of Indian removal is almost always described in the worst possible light made it encumbent upon me to attempt what I hope is a more balanced statement concerning Jackson's role in developing his Indian policy and in carrying it through the Congress to a successful conclusion. At least that is my intention, although I recognize that my view is biased in Jackson's favor and for that reason may be suspect. I myself can appreciate this difficulty, for removal was indeed a dreadful and bloody event that disgraced the nation and made a mockery of its noblest ideals.

There was another reason for including Indian removal, and that was my wish to gather into one place a detailed statement about Jackson's policy, behavior, and attitude toward Native Americans. I have written and discoursed upon the subject many times and in many different places, and I felt it was beholden upon me to attempt a synthesis of the problem as I saw it. My Jackson biography contains much of what I feel needs to be said, including an account of Jackson's actual warfare against the Indians, but that narrative is broken into three different volumes and within each volume is disbursed over several hundred pages. At least here I could gather everything that I wanted to say about Indian removal and make it generally available to anyone who might find it useful.

The slavery question is trickier. With all the attention that the subject has received over the past decade and more, it is not easy to say anything particularly new or provocative. Still it seemed important to attempt a definition of Jackson's position on the subject (and that of his friends), because of the persistence of the argument in various places that the Democratic party was the proslavery party in the antebellum period and actively advanced the southern position on the question. Indeed, it has been argued that the origins of the Democratic party were rooted in the determination of some men to build a strong bulwark around the "peculiar institution." I find this interpretation in conflict not only with contemporary sources on the principles, objectives, and desires of the party but also with the recorded intentions of those most responsible for the party's formation. Furthermore, such an interpretation is a simplistic response to an important and complicated issue that stubbornly resisted resolution. The question was not only political and economic but constitutional, moral, and psychological.

Historians have generally been aware of the Jacksonian concern for the safety of the Union if the slavery issue assumed national prominence. What they have not always realized was the fear Jacksonians had for the future of the democratic impulse sweeping the country at the time if slavery was allowed to dominate public discourse. To their mind, slavery was simply a stalking horse for those who wished to terminate majority rule by confounding the government in a brouhaha over slavery. Many of the things they feared as a consequence of a struggle over the issue did in fact occur immediately after the Civil War—just as they predicted.

The Jacksonian legacy with respect to the slavery issue is unfortunate. It is unfortunate not because they actively defended and advanced the institution, but because they tried to hide it and dismiss it, because they had no answer for the problem and would not address it properly, and because of their concern for what might happen to the country and its other institutions if the issue was allowed open discussion.

Thus, it must be admitted at the very outset that Jackson's legacy, like the legacy of most men, is a combination of good and bad, and this book seeks to demonstrate both without being all-encompassing. What I have tried to do is address three of the most important issues and events in the middle period of American history and examine Jackson's role in their development and definition. I also hope I have evoked some of the spirit and mood that Jackson reflected and indeed created during the years of his active political life. Above all, I trust it is clear that he substantially advanced the spirit of democracy in the nation and added grace and vigor to the presidential office. That in itself is a legacy for all generations.

I ❦ Democracy

The central question of the Jacksonian period in American history in my view does not focus upon slavery or western migration or the development of an industrial society—however important those questions might be—but rather upon how and by what means the United States became a democracy, upon the manner in which the doctrines of democracy replaced the doctrines of republicanism. If today this country is a democracy, how and when did it become one? For surely the Founding Fathers never envisioned that a democracy would result from their deliberations in Philadelphia in 1787.

Most thoughtful Americans are generally aware of the concern the Founders felt about overconcentrated power in a central government, a concern that reflected their desire to protect and preserve American freedom. It is also generally known that they devised a system of checks and balances to prevent such concentration. But just as they feared the exercise of power by a strong government, they also feared the exercise of power by an absolute majority and thus built safeguards against democracy into their governmental process. They created an electoral college to filter the choice of president; they conferred the election of United States senators upon state governments; they established a Supreme Court whose members would be appointed by the president with senatorial consent; and they permitted the Congress to establish inferior federal courts as needed. All judges would have life tenure provided they avoided high crimes and misdemeanors.

This is not to deny that strong elements of democracy were also embedded in the governmental system, such as the conviction that legitimate government exists by virtue of the consent of the governed. Still, what the Founders succeeded in establishing was a republic that sought to strike a balance between a powerful and a weak central government. There was a constant fear—reflected in their writings and the writings of the following generation—that those who exercised power naturally inclined toward increasing it and thereby endangered individual freedom. The struggle between liberty and power was perpetual and demanded the constant vigil of all freemen.

Between 1787, when the Founders wrote the Constitution under the guidance of principles generally called "republicanism," which they believed provided safeguards against the dangers of democracy, and the end of Andrew Jackson's administration as president in 1837, something very profound happened in the American system of government.[1] By 1837 the word *democracy* had largely supplanted the term *republicanism* in national discourse. In an essay written in 1840 for the *Democratic Review*, its editor, John L. O'Sullivan, analyzed the significance of democracy in shaping the nation without once referring to republicanism. The substitution of the ideas of democracy for those of republicanism, according to one recent historian, was "underway by the 1830s," and it would seem, therefore, that this substitution, to a very large extent, resulted from the efforts of Andrew Jackson and a number of his friends.[2] Put another way, the substitution occurred because Jackson and company—and most particularly Jackson—deliberately worked to bring about that substitution. His messages to Congress and other official statements were saturated with the single idea that the majority of people have a right and duty to govern this nation.

This occurred because Andrew Jackson was an ideologue. True, Old Hickory is not normally regarded as adhering to any firm philosophy of government. Many historians (wrongly) see his actions as motivated by private animosities and deep-

1. On republicanism see Gordon Wood, *The Creation of the American Republic, 1776–1787* (Chapel Hill, 1969); Robert E. Shalhope, "Toward a Republican Synthesis: The Emergence of an Understanding of Republicanism in American Historiography," *William and Mary Quarterly*, XXIX (1972), 49–80; Bernard Bailyn, *The Ideological Origins of the American Revolution* (Cambridge, Mass., 1967) and *The Origins of American Politics* (New York, 1968); and Joyce Appleby, "The Social Origins of American Revolutionary Ideology," *Journal of American History*, LXIV (1978), 938–40.
2. O'Sullivan's failure to mention republicanism is noted in Marcus Cunliffe's paper "The Widening and Weakening of Republicanism in Nineteenth Century America," read at the American Historical Association's annual convention, December, 1982, Washington, D.C.

seated prejudices, by passion and pride. Such an interpretation does him a grave injustice, distorts the historical record, and makes it more difficult to understand the process by which the United States advanced from republic to democracy.[3]

It is probably true that most men in politics prior to the Jacksonian age were ideologues of one kind or another. Because of their political convictions, they sided with one or the other party, either the Republican party of Jefferson and Madison or the Federalist party of Washington, Hamilton, and Adams. With the Jacksonian age, however, political parties took on a life of their own, and more and more men joined a party for reasons that had nothing to do with their political creed. In one sense Andrew Jackson is the last of the great ideologues of the early national period of American history.

That is not to say, of course, that the tenets of republicanism vanished. Many of those tenets continued throughout the nineteenth century and beyond;[4] nor should it be forgotten that republicanism informed the actions of Jackson during his tenure in the White House.[5] He doggedly clung to some of these ideas to the end of his life, for they had been formed early in his career and never left him. When he first entered politics, he fell under the influence of two extremely conservative Republicans: Representatives Nathaniel Macon of North Carolina and Henry Tazewell of Virginia. Both men advocated the rights of the states and constantly warned against the dangers inherent in a strong central government. "My political creed," Jackson admitted in 1826, "was formed in the old republican school."[6]

3. It would be invidious to single out any particular work in this regard. Suffice it to say that the "consensus school" of American historians has adopted this view.

4. Cunliffe discusses this point in his paper "The Widening and Weakening of Republicanism" and defines some of these tenets.

5. Richard Latner, *The Presidency of Andrew Jackson: White House Politics, 1829–1836* (Athens, 1979) persuasively demonstrates how indebted the Jacksonians were to the ideas of republicanism.

6. Andrew Jackson to James K. Polk, December 4, 1826, in James K. Polk Papers, Library of Congress. One can go back as far as 1797, if not earlier, to find examples of Jackson's commitment to what he called "the old republican school." See Jackson to John Sevier, February 27, 1797, in Emil Hurja Collection, Tennessee Historical Society, Nashville. The allegiance to this school is also reaffirmed in Jackson to Auguste Davezac, May 4, 1828, in Edward Livingston Papers, John R. Delafield Foundation, New York, New York.

As the first expression of his political principles, Jackson affirmed the conservative doctrine of limited government. Like Macon and Tazewell, he opposed a strong government in Washington and decried any attempt to broadly define constitutional power. He feared the danger to liberty by an energetic and omnipotent state. He worried over government interference in the lives of ordinary citizens. Government should stand clear of the normal functions of society, he said, and it must not intrude in the affairs and operations of individual states. He summoned up his thinking on this point quite early in his life when he wrote to Governor John Sevier of Tennessee: "The moment the Sovereignity [sic] of the Individual States, is overwhelmed by the General Government, we may bid adieu to our freedom."[7]

Jackson's concern over the development of a powerful central government in this country emanated from both his fear that it jeopardized the freedom of the individual and the sovereign states and his fear that centralization generated elitism, which excited the interest and attention of the rich because of the economic benefits it produced. Government then becomes the instrument of the wealthy to increase their wealth at the expense of those less fortunate. They corrupt the republican process of self-government to establish elitist rule, so that the benefits of government would be theirs exclusively. Ultimately, he said, a powerful central government "is calculated to raise around the administration a moneyed aristocracy dangerous to the liberties of the country." Thus, in Jackson's mind, a strong, overactive government threatened liberty and fostered the creation of a "moneyed aristocracy." Both as governor of the Florida Territory, and later as president, Jackson repeatedly argued that there must be "no distinction between the rich and poor the great and ignoble."[8]

Similarly, Jackson condemned the existence of a national debt. It constituted a danger to free government and served only the interest of the creditor class. Worse, that creditor class generally included the British and French, who would fatten their treasuries from the revenues collected from the great

---

7. Jackson to Sevier, February 27, 1797, in Hurja Collection.
8. Jackson to L. H. Coleman, April 26, 1824, Jackson to John Quincy Adams, November 22, 1821, in John Spencer Bassett (ed.), *Correspondence of Andrew Jackson* (Washington, D.C., 1926–33), III, 250, 139.

mass of Americans. A national debt, he wrote in 1824, is "a national curse, [and] my vow [if elected President] shall be to pay the national debt, to prevent a monied aristocracy from growing up around our administration that must bend it to its views, and ultimately destroy the liberty of our country."[9] This desire to rid the nation of debt was a very real concern to Jackson, and as president he made it one of his major objectives and major achievements. To eliminate the debt totally, of course, meant going on a tight budget, reducing government expenditures. It meant holding government spending to an absolute minimum commensurate with the safety of the nation and the performance of the duties required by the Constitution. It meant holding public works by the federal government to a minimum. In fact, Jackson actually believed that the involvement of the central government in public works was unconstitutional and that if the people really wanted them, they should address their wishes to the states or amend the Constitution to permit assumption of this responsibility by the central government. Finally, Jackson's political creed dictated that the federal government withdraw from the private sectors of the economy — withdraw from banking, for example, in which it had been involved since the rechartering of the Bank of the United States in 1816. Banking is the province of commerce, he declared, not government.[10]

There are strange, seemingly contradictory, aspects to Jackson's political thinking. For example, despite his commitment to states' rights, he was totally and passionately devoted to the Union. Although jealous of western prerogatives, sympathetic to the "peculiar institution" of the South, and sensitive (if not suspicious) of eastern presumption, Jackson exuded a brand of nationalism that was total and fanatical in its embrace of the concept of an indivisible confederation of states. This patriotic and nationalistic fervor undoubtedly took shape and form in his youth. He was a product of the Revolutionary generation. As a boy he fought in the Revolution, during which he was captured by the British, scarred for life on his head and wrist by a British soldier for refusing a menial task, imprisoned, nearly killed by smallpox, and, ultimately, devastated by the loss of

9. Jackson to William S. Fulton, July 4, 1824, in *ibid.*, III, 259.
10. Robert V. Remini, *Andrew Jackson and the Course of American Freedom, 1822–1832* (New York, 1981), 34ff.

his immediate family. After the Revolution, by the time he journeyed to Tennessee as a young lawyer in pursuit of a new life in the West, Jackson had developed into a fierce nationalist whose concern for freedom was as total as his love of the Union. He had long arrived at the conclusion that individual freedom was best protected by a strong, united nation. "There is nothing that I shudder at more than the idea of a seperation of the Union," he wrote. "Should such an event ever happen, which I fervently pray god to avert, from that date, I view our liberty gone."[11] He still believed in limited government because he recognized that powerful governments could also jeopardize freedom. Thus, as a counterweight to centralized government he championed the rights of the states.[12]

Jackson himself matured on the frontier as both an ideologue and a political leader. His service as an Indian fighter in company with small bands of other Tennesseans honed his skills as a leader. Participating in the settlement of the territory and helping to write Tennessee's constitution, as well as serving in the Congress as his state's first member of the House of Representatives, he learned the importance and necessity of free elections. "The great constitutional corrective in the hands of the people against usurpation of power, or corruption by their agents," he said, "is the right of suffrage; and this when used with calmness and deliberation will prove strong enough. It will perpetuate their liberties and rights."[13]

Like all believers in republicanism, Jackson recognized and argued that liberty had as its greatest bulwark the virtue of a free people. And it was only the virtue of the people that sustained and protected their republican system of government. Once virtue fled, free government ceased to exist. "My fervent prayers," he said in 1822, "are that our republican government may be perpetual, and the people alone by their Virtue, and

11. Jackson to James Hamilton, Jr., June 29, 1828, in Bassett (ed.), *Correspondence of Andrew Jackson*, III, 412.
12. On Jackson's early career there are two sources, apart from the documents themselves, that are valuable: James Parton, *Life of Andrew Jackson* (3 vols.; New York, 1861); and Amos Kendall, *The Life of Andrew Jackson* (New York, 1844). On Jackson's military career see John Reid and John Henry Eaton, *The Life of Andrew Jackson* (Philadelphia, 1817).
13. Jackson to James Buchanan, June 25, 1825, in James Buchanan Papers, Historical Society of Pennsylvania, Philadelphia.

independent exercise of their free suffrage can make it perpetual."[14]

The danger to liberty, according to the adherents of republicanism, was the misuse of power. King George III had misused his authority by appointing officials who sought to corrupt the representatives elected by the people in their assemblies. And as virtue served to bulwark liberty, corruption augmented the misuse of power. The struggle between liberty and power had produced the American Revolution and ultimately independence for the patriot cause. But the danger to freedom was ever present, and only the virtue of the people could shield it from extinction.

Jackson developed into an ideologue not because of profound immersion in the writings of political scientists. His thinking developed out of an unusual personal history that favored him with a wide range of experiences, both political and economic. His was not so much a coherent and consistent philosophy of government as it was a set of convictions that he regarded as absolute. Some of these convictions reflect his southern and western background; others his Scotch-Irish heritage; still others his Presbyterian upbringing.

In the evolution of Jackson's thinking about republicanism and democracy there was a single event that exercised more influence on him in shaping his political thoughts than anything else in his entire political life. That event provides a convenient turning point in the evolution of the country from a republic to a democracy, for it set in motion new and powerful forces and resolute men who deliberately sought to change the political operation of the country. That event was remembered by Jackson to his dying day, and it was referred to and reiterated by him ceaselessly. It was also cited and wrung through a thousand different changes by his friends to wreak political havoc upon their opponents. Unquestionably, it was one of the most significant political events in the entire antebellum period. And that event was the presidential election of 1824–1825, when John Quincy Adams, with the considerable assistance of Henry Clay, was chosen president of the United States

14. Jackson to Andrew Jackson Donelson, August 6, 1822, in Andrew Jackson Donelson Papers, Library of Congress.

by the House of Representatives over Andrew Jackson and William H. Crawford.[15]

The so-called "corrupt bargain" between Clay and Adams that worked to their immediate advantage and subsequent defeat did more than simply unite the friends of Jackson and give them a rallying cry by which to defeat the Adams-Clay coalition in 1828.[16] It provided the gospel by which an entire generation interpreted the role of government and the relationship between the central government in Washington and the mass electorate. It was the single event that drove men—Jackson especially—to a more pronounced democratic position and ended forever the notion that representatives are somehow free agents to decide by themselves the public good.

The election of 1824–1825 unleashed the democratic storm that had been building for years—if not decades—and radically changed the system of government in all its branches as well as between constituencies. Moreover, it provided the philosophic basis by which the American electorate viewed and interpreted government and its functions.

Jackson personally was scalded by the election. Like most men of his age, he had regarded the legislature as the best instrument for the protection of liberty. Now he knew better. The House election completely disabused him of that idea. In his mind the legislature had failed its primary purpose. "The people [have] been cheated," he reportedly said. "Corruptions and intrigues at Washington . . . defeated the will of the people."[17]

In creating a two-house legislature under the Constitution, with the lower house elected directly by the people and the upper house by the states, the Founding Fathers believed that they had effected a balance that would prevent tyranny and anarchy and thereby safeguard freedom. Thus, it seemed appropriate that when the two political parties of the 1790s, the Federalists and Republicans, came to decide which candidates to run for the executive branch, the members of each party in

15. James F. Hopkins, "Election of 1824," in Arthur M. Schlesinger, Jr., and Fred L. Israel (eds.), *History of American Presidential Elections* (4 vols.; New York, 1971), I, 349–81 offers the best account of this election.

16. On the election of 1828 see Robert V. Remini, *The Election of Andrew Jackson* (New York, 1963).

17. *Niles' Weekly Register*, July 5, 1828.

Congress would caucus and select their respective favorites. A congressional caucus, as the instrument of presidential nominations, had been in operation for several decades when Jackson returned to the political scene. Presumably what had been acceptable to Jefferson and Madison and Monroe should also serve Andrew Jackson.

But circumstances had changed when Jackson decided to run for the presidency in 1824. The Federalist party was all but extinct on the national level, and Jefferson's Republican party reigned supreme.[18] Thus, the candidate for the presidency put forward by the Republican party would win the office by default. There was no contest. The election of the president was virtually assigned to a small group of politicians meeting in a congressional caucus. The College of Electors would then place the stamp of approval upon that choice. Although congressional caucuses for purposes of nomination were not unusual, at least in the past a political contest between two candidates representing the different parties had always ensued. At least the electorate had made the final selection. Now there was only one party and (presumably) one candidate. That fact should have rendered a congressional caucus totally improper—or so said Andrew Jackson and others in 1824. "[I] will save the nation from the rule of Demagogues," the general told his wife, "who by intrigue are, & have been attempting to cheat the people out of their constitutional rights, by a caucus of congressional members."[19] To Jackson a caucus to select the president negated the idea of free elections. For a select body of congressmen, rather than the American people, to decide the presidential question was a gross violation of the constitutional system. Moreover, everyone knew that the decision of the caucus was preordained and that William H. Crawford of Georgia, the secretary of the treasury, would receive the

---

18. The history of these early parties can be traced in the following works: Noble E. Cunningham, *The Jeffersonian Republicans* (Chapel Hill, 1957); Joseph Carles, *The Origins of the American Party System* (Williamsburg, 1956); Norman Risjord, *The Early American Party System* (New York, 1969); Roy Nichols, *The Invention of the American Party System* (New York, 1967); Morton Borden, *Parties and Politics in the Early Republic, 1789–1815* (New York, 1963); and William Chambers, *Political Parties in a New Nation* (New York, 1963).
19. Jackson to Rachel Jackson, February 6, 1824, in Andrew Jackson Papers, Huntington Library, San Marino, California.

nomination on account of his popularity among congressmen and the excellence of his political operation in Washington.[20]

Thus, it appeared to many people that Congress was about to remove the presidential election from the control of the electorate. And suspicion turned to certainty when Crawford suffered a stroke that paralyzed him and yet congressmen continued to organize their caucus for him anyway. They were intent on lifting to the presidency a man who could not perform his duties, one paralyzed, sightless, and dumb.

Despite mounting criticism, the call went out for a caucus to be held in the chamber of the House of Representatives on Saturday, February 14, 1824. Senator Martin Van Buren of New York organized and directed the meeting, but only sixty-six congressmen honored his call, less than a quarter of the combined members of the two houses. Not to be denied their "right" to put forward a national nominee, the members assembled, selected a chairman and secretary, and proceeded to vote, oblivious to the cries from the gallery that they adjourn. When the balloting ended, Chairman Benjamin Ruggles of Ohio announced that Crawford had received 62 votes, Adams 25, and Jackson and Nathaniel Macon 1 each; by proxy, 2 additional votes were awarded to Crawford. It was then declared "to the heavy groans in the Gallery" that William H. Crawford of Georgia was the official standard-bearer of the Republican party.[21]

Any number of other ambitious politicians raised their voices in protest over this singular mockery of democratic procedure, and a few of them ultimately won presidential nominations from their respective states. What finally resulted was a four-way contest between Adams, Jackson, Clay, and Crawford in which no candidate received a required majority of electoral votes. However, Jackson obtained a plurality of both the popular and electoral votes. To many Americans, therefore, the public had spoken its will as best it could, and to them it seemed that the House of Representatives should choose Jackson as the next president in deference to that will.[22]

---

20. For a biography of Crawford, see Chase C. Mooney, *William H. Crawford, 1772–1834* (Lexington, Ky., 1974).

21. Robert V. Remini, *Martin Van Buren and the Making of the Democratic Party* (New York, 1959), 47–50.

22. Van Buren's role in this election can be traced in two excellent biogra-

But that is not what happened. As was their constitutional right, the House of Representatives set aside the perceived "will of the people" and elected John Quincy Adams as the nation's sixth president. In more than thirty-five years of republican rule under the Constitution nothing like this had ever happened before. The nation had veered very close to such a constitutional crisis in the election of 1800–1801, when Jefferson and Aaron Burr received a tie vote in the electoral college. Fortunately, the House elected Jefferson, which the electorate undoubtedly wanted and expected. It can be easily imagined what a furor would have ensued had Burr been elevated to the presidency.

One of the striking differences between the 1800 and 1824 elections is that a popular vote had been registered (however limited) in 1824. The members of Congress had a reasonably clear idea who the American people favored in the latter election. And although Jackson had fewer popular votes than the *combined* tally of his opponents—153,000 to 208,000—he did have the plurality—more than anyone else.[23] To set that result aside did seem to some, especially the Jacksonians, like a denial of "democratic" rule. But these congressmen who voted in the House election, it must be remembered, felt no compulsion to abide by democratic rule. Many of them feared and distrusted democracy and felt a greater obligation to protect and defend the doctrines of republicanism. And under a republican system they had the right—and it was a constitutional right—to choose the next president from among the three candidates with the highest electoral vote. Thus, prior to 1824 the nation espoused what might be loosely defined as republican doctrines, republican attitudes, and republican sentiment. After 1825 there is a sharp swing toward democratic doctrines, democratic attitudes, and democratic sentiment. This democratic swing is part of the legacy of Andrew Jackson.

Jackson's arrival on the national political scene accelerated the development of a democratic system in the United States.

---

phies: John Niven, *Martin Van Buren: The Romantic Age of American Politics* (New York, 1983); and Donald B. Cole, *Martin Van Buren and the American Political System* (Princeton, 1984).

23. Hopkins, "Election of 1824," in Schlesinger and Israel (eds.), *History of American Presidential Elections*, I, 371.

Today it is most unlikely that anyone would dare to set aside the popular will in a presidential election even if it did follow constitutional form. It was reported that President Gerald Ford in 1976 considered challenging certain electoral returns that might have given him the electoral college majority. But he decided against such a challenge because he would still have lacked a popular majority and he knew he risked grave consequences if he fought to win the presidency on the basis of the electoral vote alone.

The Jacksonians not only registered their displeasure over the rejection of their candidate in 1825 but charged a "corrupt bargain" between Adams and Clay to subvert the popular will. Whether Adams ever promised Clay an appointment as secretary of state in exchange for House votes that would lift him into the White House, as the Jacksonians subsequently charged, is irrelevant.[24] Far more important is the fact that Adams, Clay, and their House supporters disregarded the declared and known intentions of the electorate.

In order to deliver Kentucky's vote in the House election, Clay had to dismiss not only the results of the contest of the previous fall but also the instructions of the Kentucky legislature to the congressional delegation that the vote of the state be cast for Jackson. The fall election in Kentucky had been a contest between Clay and Jackson. No one else was involved. According to the official count, Adams never received a single vote in Kentucky. Clearly, the people of that state wanted a westerner as their president. To award Adams the vote of Kentucky in the House, therefore, was seen as contemptuous of the popular will and a gross violation of Kentucky's right to have its vote cast for the candidate of its choice. No one denied that the House members of the Kentucky delegation had a constitutional right to vote for whomever they wished. But in exercising that right by voting for a man who could not attract a single popular vote from their constituency, they expressed their indifference to the wishes of the electorate—and not only

24. I am more and more convinced that the two men did reach an understanding of sorts, although they probably did it in a noncompromising way. In his journal Adams is careful about what he reveals concerning his meeting with Clay. See Charles Francis Adams (ed.), *Memoirs of John Quincy Adams* (12 vols.; Philadelphia, 1874–77), VI, 458ff. An excellent recent study, *The Presidency of John Quincy Adams* (Lawrence, 1985) by Mary W. M. Hargreaves, fails to settle the question of the "corrupt bargain."

the electorate, but the legislature as well. The House members from Kentucky had explicit instructions to vote for "the regional candidate," and Jackson was the only one who fitted that description. They chose to turn a deaf ear to the legislature and listen instead to Clay. "Thus you see here," growled the outraged Jackson, "the voice of the people of the west have been disregarded, and demagogues barter them as sheep in the shambles, for their own views, and personal agrandisement."[25]

To gain the Missouri vote in the House election, Adams personally violated a federal statute by agreeing not to remove a federal judge who had participated in a duel. The judge in question served in the Arkansas Territory and had killed a colleague in a duel. Since territorial law forbade duelists from holding office, the judge should have been removed. And in fact an application for removal had already been initiated, but it had not been acted upon. So the judge's brother, John Scott, who just happened to be Missouri's single representative in the House of Representatives, went to John Q. Adams and asked him what he would do in his brother's case if he were elected president. Adams assured him that his brother would keep his position. Thomas Hart Benton, the senator from Missouri, tried to convince Scott that it was his duty to vote for Jackson, since "nine tenths of the people" in the West were known to be "decidedly in [Jackson's] favor."[26] But Scott paid no mind to this argument and handed Missouri over to Adams. In the next election Scott was overwhelmingly defeated, and he never again returned to public office. As for the brother, Adams not only kept him on the bench but renominated him when his four-year term expired. However, the Senate rejected the nomination as a gross violation of the law.[27] Scott, it should be reiterated, had every constitutional right to vote for Adams, but his actions and those of Adams were seen as a moral subversion of the Constitution and a denial of popular rule.

The House election of 1825 that awarded the presidency to

25. Remini, *Jackson and the Course of American Freedom*, 179–95; Jackson to John Overton, February 10, 1825, in John Overton Papers, Tennessee Historical Society, Nashville.
26. Benton's account of the election can be found in his *Thirty Years' View* (2 vols.; New York, 1865), I, 46ff.
27. Samuel Flagg Bemis, *John Quincy Adams and the Union* (New York, 1956), II, 42–43; Adams (ed.), *Memoirs of J. Q. Adams*, VI, 443, 473–475.

John Quincy Adams had a profound impact on Jackson's thinking. Unquestionably, it was *the* single event—if single events in history actually do determine actions by themselves—that converted him into a rabid democrat, that is, into one who passionately believed in the need for majority rule, the right of the people acting through the ballot box to decide "upon all national or general subjects, as well as local."[28] Henceforth he preached a remarkably advanced form of democracy and argued that it provided the surest means of protecting individual rights. No longer could the legislature be trusted to serve the popular will. It had repeatedly demonstrated its capacity for corruption. The electorate would have to look elsewhere.

The entire democratic thrust of the Jacksonian era finds its real beginnings in the 1824–1825 presidential election and the effect that election had upon General Jackson and the other leaders of the Democratic party. Notice his actions throughout his two terms in office. All his political battles ring with a democratic cry. Unfortunately, some historians are prone to hear only the sounds of an outraged egomaniac. They frequently miss the more essential voice about the nature of the American experiment in government. Moreover—and this is equally important—all his political battles have an ideological core, usually reflecting his commitment to the early philosophy of republicanism, especially states' rights, or his deep concern for the rights and welfare of the people.[29]

As an ideologue, of course, Jackson cannot compare with Jefferson, Madison, Hamilton, or the other great men of the Revolutionary generation. He simply does not have their learning or intellectual depth. But his thinking about representative government is far more advanced than theirs—more advanced, indeed, than Americans of the present day. He pushed the concept of democracy about as far as it can go and still remain workable.

What historians have often failed to notice in their disdain of this ill-tutored, violent, rabble-rousing "frontiersman" is that

28. Jackson to Donelson, May 12, 1835, in Donelson Papers.
29. Shalhope, "Toward a Republican Synthesis," 49–80; Latner, *Presidency of Jackson*, 3, 11, 13, 23–25, 209–12; Remini, *Jackson and the Course of American Freedom*, 26ff; Robert P. Hay, "The Case for Andrew Jackson in 1824: Eaton's *Wyoming Letters*," *Tennessee Historical Quarterly*, XXIX (1970), 140–49.

most of Jackson's political battles involve a moral issue expressed in populistic terms. The Jacksonian age begins with a shout of moral outrage. "The will of the people has been thwarted," Jackson thundered in anger over the "corrupt bargain." "The *Judas* of the West," as he called Henry Clay, "has closed the contract and will receive the thirty pieces of silver. His end will be the same. Was there ever witnessed such a bare faced corruption in any country before?"[30] This moral tone can be heard again and again throughout his entire administration. Rotation — or "the spoils system" as his enemies preferred to call it — was intended to root out corruption in public office and restore honesty to government, however else his enemies chose to interpret it. And in the Bank War, Jackson always expressed his view of the struggle in both democratic and moral terms, specifically as a struggle of honest workers against corrupt aristocrats, between the many and the few, between the laboring poor and those who would exploit them. In the nullification controversy, he said he would build a moral force throughout the country and through its instrumentality save the Union and put down treason and insurrection. And in Indian removal he always insisted that his policy was intended to save Indians from inevitable extinction.

Acknowledging the moral dimension of the major issues of the Jackson presidency — and this would include even the notorious Eaton affair, in which the president made a national issue out of the discourtesies shown to John H. Eaton's wife, Peggy, by members of his cabinet and other prominent Washingtonians — has nothing to do with Jackson's own personal morality or that of members of his administration. No religious convictions are implied. Some Americans find Jackson's own habits of temperament — his vindictiveness, for example, and his violent temper when provoked — disturbing and distasteful, and for them any intimation of morality connected with his administration is ludicrous. That Old Hickory would define national issues in moral terms says more about his political sense than his own commitment to religious or moral ideals. A shrewd politician who instinctively reacted to men and ideas as a leader of the entire electorate, he not only

30. Jackson to William B. Lewis, February 14, 1825, in Bassett (ed.), *Correspondence of Jackson*, III, 276.

quickly identified the moral dimension in most issues, but he actively searched for it.[31] Thus, Jackson's populistic approach to political questions continues to be a vital force throughout American history. And this is part of his legacy to the nation.

Not only Jackson himself, but the Democratic party, which was founded at this time and organized around his appeal to the American people, benefited from identification with a moral purpose. From the beginning of its history the Democratic party appeared to rest on a moral base. The party emerged fully developed, so to speak, during the Bank War, and that war was waged on the premise — whether it was true or not — that the rich business classes were robbing the poor working classes and needed to be stopped and would be stopped by the champions of the people (the Democrats) led by the Old Hero of the Battle of New Orleans, Andrew Jackson. The Democratic party from its inception was ostensibly committed to the concerns of the masses of people. It claimed the allegiance of the largest numbers of people from every class and section of the nation. Jackson himself always insisted that he spoke for and represented the majority of Americans,[32] that he stood for their interests against the interests of the few, that he resisted the greed and corruption of the wealthy elite. Said one of his critics: The American people believed that President Jackson was "honest and patriotic; that he was the friend of the *people*, battling for them against corruption and extravagance, and opposed only by dishonest politicians. They loved him as their friend."[33] Whether his claims — and they *are* extravagant — were true or not is beside the point. Many, if not most, people believed him.

In his political crusades he summoned the electorate to support his cause. He invariably called on the people to join him in

31. Robert V. Remini, *Andrew Jackson and the Bank War* (New York, 1967); Robert V. Remini, *Andrew Jackson and the Course of American Democracy, 1833–1845* (New York, 1984), 9–10, 314.

32. Jackson argues this position most effectively in his "Protest" message to the Senate dated April 15, 1834. See J. D. Richardson (comp.), *Compilation of the Messages and Papers of the Presidents, 1782–1892* (Washington, D.C., 1908), II, 1289ff.

33. Nathan Sargent, *Public Men and Events* (2 vols.; Philadelphia, 1875), I, 347.

his efforts on their behalf. And they responded in overwhelming numbers. Jackson, in effect, loosed the power of the masses, something never done before in American history. In releasing that power, he necessarily delivered a crushing blow to republicanism, at least those aspects of it that resisted the notion of majoritarian rule. For Jackson there was never any question that democracy consisted of rule by the majority. Unlike many of the Founding Fathers, whose political faith rested squarely on republicanism, he did not fear democratic rule. In the *Federalist* no. 10, James Madison wrote that "democracies have ever been spectacles of turbulence and contention; have ever been found incompatible with personal security or the rights of property; and have in general been as short in their lives as they have been violent in their deaths." This rather jaundiced view of democracy did not reflect Jackson's thinking. Quite the contrary. "The people are the government," he wrote, "administering it by their agents; they are the Government, the sovereign power." In his first inaugural address he stated his basic position once and for all: "The majority is to govern," he declared.[34]

When Jackson first arrived in Washington in 1829 to assume leadership of the country as president, he declared his intention of pursuing a program of "reform retrenchment and economy" by which he would restore the nation and its government to virtue and honesty.[35] In his inaugural address on March 4, 1829, and in his first message to Congress in December, 1829, he particularized his intentions by calling for a policy of rotation in office, the removal of the Indians, alterations in the charter of the Bank of the United States in order to improve the nation's currency and credit facilities, and other items dealing with the tariff and internal improvements. But encapsulating the whole was a general sense of the need to make the government more responsive to the perceived needs of the American people, in short to institute democratic government.[36] The rhetoric of

34. Jackson to Donelson, May 12, 1835, in Donelson Papers; Richardson (comp.), *Messages and Papers of the Presidents*, II, 1011.
35. "Outline of Principles Submitted to the Heads of Departments," February 23, 1829, in Andrew Jackson Papers, Library of Congress.
36. Richardson (comp.), *Messages and Papers of the Presidents*, II, 1011ff.

Jacksonian propaganda—led and sometimes initiated by the president himself, especially in his mouthpiece, the Washington *Globe*, and in his messages to Congress and other state papers—was saturated with democratic intent. "The people are sovereign," Old Hickory kept insisting in his public addresses; "their will is absolute."[37] And his intent in speaking in this fashion was not pragmatic. This was not political rhetoric to win votes. Rather it was the expression of a genuinely felt belief that the life of the Republic depended totally on popular rule.

This was a new concept in American politics. In writing the Constitution, the Founding Fathers had agreed that a just government was based on the consent of the governed, but that did not necessarily translate into democratic rule. Madison, again in the *Federalist* no. 10, argued for a republic in which public views could be filtered through "the medium of a chosen body of citizens" whose wisdom, patriotism, and love of justice would best discern what was in the country's genuine interests. Madison regarded democracy as an "unstable" effort to include every citizen in the operation of government. What needed to be avoided, he warned, was such undesirable features of popular government as majority rule. For majority rule, he averred, could jeopardize the personal and property rights of the minority. When the common good dictated another course of action than that determined by the majority, the Revolutionary generation felt completely free to make decisions contrary to the will of the majority. Thus, the choice of John Quincy Adams in the House election of 1825 was fully in accord with this philosophy. Moreover, any number of Revolutionary fathers argued that the language of the Constitution *is* in fact the will of the people. Having spoken in adopting the Constitution, the masses are excluded from directly speaking again except through the difficult, if not impossible, process of amending the instrument.[38] The branch of government that has the right to determine the final meaning of the Constitution is the Supreme Court. And the Supreme Court, as the Founders well knew, was the body most removed from the peo-

37. These expressions can also be found in his private correspondence. See, for example, Jackson to Donelson, May 12, 1835, in Donelson Papers.

38. This point is splendidly developed in John William Ward's article "Jacksonian Democratic Thought: 'A Natural Charter of Privilege,'" in Stanley Coben and Lorman Ratner (eds.), *The Development of an American Culture* (New York, 1983), 58–79.

ple, and it remains so. The Supreme Court represents the intrusion of aristocratic or oligarchic rule into the American system of government. But the Founding Fathers were not attempting to eliminate aristocratic government. They believed in a mixed government with elements of aristocratic, republican, and democratic forms embedded in the whole.

This view, this philosophy, this type of government Andrew Jackson totally rejected. Not only did he deny that the electorate may intrude no more except by amending the Constitution, he also denied that the Supreme Court was the final interpreter of the meaning of the Constitution—a view denounced even today by many liberal thinkers. In justifying his veto of the bill to renew the charter of the Bank of the United States, Jackson wrote: "It is maintained by the advocates of the Bank that its constitutionality . . . ought to be considered as settled . . . by the decision of the Supreme Court. To this conclusion I can not assent. . . . The authority of the Supreme Court must not be permitted to control the Congress or the Executive when acting in their legislative capacities, but to have only such influence as the force of their reasoning may deserve."[39]

Jackson's view of the American system of government was completely different from the Founding Fathers', and far more democratic. First of all, he maintained that the people always remain active in the governing process. The people can *never* be excluded; they did not surrender their right of self-government when they adopted the Constitution. They exercise it regularly through the ballot box, which all agencies of government (including the Supreme Court) must obey. Otherwise the Supreme Court, by a majority of four men in the 1830s—men who were not necessarily the most learned in the law and had won their seat by political appointment, not election—might dictate to millions. That was not democracy. Nor was it republican. It was oligarchy, said Jackson, and unacceptable in a free nation. A form of government such as the one provided by the Constitution does not divest the people of the right to self-government. It does not give the Supreme Court the right to tell them what is or is not allowed under that form. "Where the people are everything, and political forms . . . nothing," wrote one Jacksonian, "there and there only is liberty."[40]

39. Richardson (comp.), *Messages and Papers of the Presidents*, II, 1144–45.
40. George Sidney Camp, *Democracy* (New York, 1841), 161–62.

The danger, of course, is that without a rule of law interpreted by a high court, the majority will tyrannize the minority. Sooner or later the property rights of the wealthy few will be placed in jeopardy, and they will have nowhere to turn for protection. But in a democracy such a risk is unavoidable. Jackson dismissed it as a real objection. He placed his entire confidence in the wisdom of a virtuous people "to arrive at right conclusions."[41] He refused to believe that "a virtuous people" in a democracy would permit tyranny.

Jackson's philosophy of government was direct and simple: the people govern. Their will must be obeyed. Majority rule constitutes the only true meaning of liberty. On every issue, he wrote, sovereign power resides with the people.[42] It does not reside with the states, and certainly not the courts. Jackson, himself a lawyer during his early years in Tennessee and a superior court judge to boot,[43] would allow the courts the right to review and interpret the *law*, but he would not assign them ultimate authority in pronouncing "the true meaning of a doubtful clause of the Constitution" that would be binding on all Americans. The right to review and interpret the law may be "endured," he reasoned, "because it is subject to the control of the majority of the people." But for the courts to pronounce the true meaning of the Constitution was altogether objectionable because "it claims the right to bind" both the states and the people in such a way that they cannot free themselves except by amending the Constitution, a difficult process at best. To allow the Supreme Court the ultimate authority to interpret the Constitution perpetuates an oligarchic rather than a democratic system of government because less than half a dozen jurists can dictate to an entire nation, with or without popular consent.[44]

41. Remini, *Jackson and the Course of American Democracy*, 338.
42. Jackson to Donelson, May 12, 1835, in Donelson Papers.
43. See Robert V. Remini, *Andrew Jackson and the Course of American Empire, 1767–1821* (New York, 1977), 37–56, 113–24.
44. These views of Jackson come from various sources, mostly his private letters (for example, his letter to Donelson, May 12, 1835, in Donelson Papers), his public papers (for example, his Bank veto message) and the editorial columns of the Washington *Globe* (for example, the issue of July 27, 1832). See also the notes of George Bancroft's interview with Jackson written by Bancroft, in Manuscript Ledger, George Bancroft Papers, Massachusetts Historical Society, Boston.

By the middle of the twentieth century the courts had assumed virtually unlimited power in practically all areas of law, social behavior, politics, economics, and every other field. Busing school children, forbidding prayers in school, and permitting abortions are just a few recent decisions that indicate the wide range of judicial involvement in social and private issues. In Illinois in 1983 Governor James Thompson vetoed a section of the budget approved by the legislature that continued the operation of several mental institutions. The governor argued that the state could not afford the expense of maintaining these institutions. A suit was immediately brought, and a judge issued a writ blocking the governor's action. Thompson angrily responded that if the courts have undertaken the responsibility of budgeting expenditures for Illinois, then the people might as well close down the legislative and executive branches of government, since there was no area of governmental activity in which the courts could not intrude and dictate a course of action.

In 1984 a three-judge federal court ruled that Louisiana could not cancel a presidential primary election to save $1.5 million, as directed by the state legislature. Like it or not, the people of Louisiana were required to hold and pay for a primary they conceivably did not want. Thus, a three-judge court arranged and dictated a political matter and a political procedure and imposed it upon a sovereign state and the people of that state without their consent.

What has developed—particularly since the Civil War—is unrestrained judicial review, an "imperial judiciary," so called. Jackson would have regarded this as "aristocratic rule," rule far more dangerous than democratic rule. He said he would take his chances with "a virtuous people" rather than an appointed court who sat for their lifetimes and answered to no one but their own individual consciences.[45]

Still, resistance to the rule of law interpreted by the courts inevitably creates serious problems. And Jackson himself fell victim to his own philosophy. He would not rely upon the courts to decide the character of abolitionist literature and therefore got tangled in a series of questions over the freedom

45. Jackson to John Coffee, April 7, 1832, in Coffee Papers, Tennessee Historical Society, Nashville; Charles J. Johnson to [?], March 23, 1832, in David Campbell Papers, Duke University Library, Durham, N.C.

of the mails. Jackson believed that the literature was wicked. He also believed it was revolutionary and unconstitutional because it fomented "servile insurrection"—slave against master. But he also believed that the mails must be delivered. Then who shall decide whether the tracts in question should be delivered if not the courts? Jackson refused to go to the courts for an opinion. But that was not unusual in the 1830s. Application for judicial decision of political and private rights, even when involving conflicting interpretation, was not accepted procedure in the early nineteenth century.[46] That developed after the Civil War. In the Jacksonian era and earlier, great reliance was placed on the legislature to come up with solutions to such problems. So Jackson asked Congress to enact legislation that would prohibit the circulation through the South of incendiary publications intended to instigate the slaves to insurrection. Unfortunately, Congress refused to oblige him. Instead the Post Office Act of 1836 forbade postmasters from detaining the delivery of mail. As a result southern postmasters regularly disregarded this legislation (with Jackson looking the other way) in the belief that federal authority over the mail ceased at the reception point. In 1857 Attorney General Caleb Cushing decided that a postmaster could refuse to deliver mail of an incendiary character but that it was up to the courts to decide what was and what was not incendiary.[47] And it should be noted that the problem involving abolitionist literature and the action by southern postmasters was not comparable with the quarrel over South Carolina's nullification of the tariff in 1832. South Carolina's action defied the established law of the land. The incident over abolitionist literature involved jurisdiction, about which there was conflicting interpretation.

A television program concerning the Constitution and entitled "The Delicate Balance" appeared not long ago, and one of the distinguished panelists was asked what he would advise the president to do if he were the attorney general and the Supreme Court, on a case brought to it by the Congress, ordered the president to remove troops from a foreign country.

46. Richardson (comp.), *Messages and Papers of the Presidents*, II, 1395; Remini, *Jackson and Course of American Democracy*, 262–63.
47. Richardson (comp.), *Messages and Papers of the Presidents*, II, 1395; Leonard D. White, *The Jacksonians: A Study in Administrative History, 1829–1861* (New York, 1954), 520.

The panelist immediately responded that he would advise the president to keep the troops where they were. Another panelist, who was a federal judge, urged the first panelist to reconsider, insisting that the American system required acceptance of the court's ruling even in a political matter. The first panelist ultimately backed down, agreeing that his advice to the president struck at the very essence of the American legal and governmental system. Yet it merits repeating that not only is this system undemocratic, but it is not what the Founding Fathers established. Nowhere in the Constitution does it say that the Supreme Court will interpret the Constitution, much less that it is the final arbiter of *all* issues, whether political, social, economic, or legal, or that the other two branches of government must obey it. On the contrary: if the Constitution says anything, it says that the three branches are equal and separate.

It has been a long time since a president defied the Supreme Court. Not even Franklin Roosevelt was guilty of this offense. He attacked the Court and threatened to pack it, but he did not defy its rulings. No doubt Richard Nixon had defiance in mind when he was instructed to hand over the tapes in the Watergate tragedy, but he had been involved in a criminal conspiracy, and he knew his impeachment was a certainty if he disobeyed the order. Nor did Jackson defy the Court. Despite his contempt of the *Worcester* decision he did not defy the Court, because there was nothing for him to defy.[48] Certainly he was capable of defiance in more ways than one. For one thing the idea of unlimited judicial review revolted him. As he said in his message on the Bank veto, he believed that "the Congress, the Executive, and the Court must each for itself be guided by its own opinion of the Constitution."[49] Of course, it is really improper to compare the legal situation in the mid-nineteenth century with that at the end of the twentieth. The application for judicial decision of political, social, and private rights in the Jacksonian age—even when involving conflicting interpreta-

48. *Worcester* v. *Georgia* was a case that involved the imprisonment of two missionaries by the state of Georgia. Jackson's response to the decision is treated at length in Remini, *Jackson and the Course of American Freedom*, 276ff. See also Edwin Miles, "After John Marshall's Decision: *Worcester* v. *Georgia* and the Nullification Crisis," *Journal of Southern History*, XXXIX (1973), 519–44.
49. Richardson (comp.), *Messages and Papers of the Presidents*, II, 1142.

tions—was virtually unknown. That trend developed only in time and after many crises and controversies, including the Civil War and its aftermath.

In view of Jackson's low opinion of the prerogatives of the Supreme Court it will readily be understood why he did *not* say: "Well: John Marshall has made his decision: *now let him enforce it!*"[50] He would not have said it, because the quotation implies that the decision of the Supreme Court is final and binding on all, including the president of the United States, and Jackson never believed or accepted that view. The quotation may indeed convey Jackson's feelings about the Court and its opinion in the *Worcester* case, but surely he would never have said anything to suggest the Court's primacy in deciding what was essentially a political issue.[51]

Not only did Jackson preach majoritarian rule in which all three branches of government must obey the will of the people; he also believed in participatory democracy as a guarantee for the preservation of liberty.[52] With the expanding economy so characteristic of the Jackson years, with rising expectations, increased social mobility, and a higher standard of living, a great many people also expected to exercise a greater voice in their government. And Jackson, in his own unique way, sought to accommodate them. In inaugurating his administration, he claimed he would institute a series of reforms that would make the government more responsive to the expressed will of the people. He began with the introduction of the principle of rotation. Despite appearances and however it actually worked in practice, rotation was never intended by its originator simply to reward the political faithful and punish their enemies. Rather it was introduced by Jackson not only to terminate a corruption he believed had long festered within the executive branch but, more important, to establish the democratic doctrine that in a free country no one has a special privilege or

50. Horace Greeley, *The American Conflict: A History of the Great Rebellion in the United States of America, 1860–'64* (2 vols.; Hartford, Conn., 1865), I, 106.

51. Lewis Williams to William Lenoir, April 9, 1832, in Miles, "After John Marshall's Decision," 533 n. 32. The *Worcester* case will be discussed at greater length in the following chapter.

52. Richardson (comp.), *Messages and Papers of the Presidents*, II, 1011–12.

right to control or run the nation.[53] Government must be open to all. There must be no elitism, no official class. All citizens, said Jackson, have a right to participate in the day-to-day function of government. It took only a few years, he said, for an officeholder to believe that "he has a life estate in it, a vested right." And if he has been in office for twenty years or more, Jackson continued, he believes not only that he has a vested right "but that it ought to descend to his children, & if no children then the next of kin. This is not the principle of our government," declared Old Hickory. "It is rotation in office that will perpetuate our liberty."[54]

He explained his principle in his first message to Congress, declaring that office is an "instrument created solely for the service of the people"; it is not a species of property. His plan[55] (although he never worked out all the details) was to limit appointment to four years. Every four years, therefore, or at the beginning of each new administration, an entirely new corps of government employees could be brought into office. This four-year limit, he said, would destroy the idea of "office-as-property" and bring many more citizens directly into government service.[56]

Historians have pointed out that Jackson's appointees hardly qualify as examples of a new democratic thrust to government office holding. In terms of their social, economic, and educational backgrounds Jackson's appointees differed hardly at all from their predecessors. Thus, government service was not really opened to the masses but rather remained with the same

53. A number of historians refuse to believe that the period prior to the Jacksonian age was as corrupt as Jackson insisted it was. Be that as it may, the important point is that Jackson himself believed it. See Remini, *Jackson and the Course of American Freedom*, 12ff. The question of corruption was examined most objectively by Richard L. McCormick in a paper read before the American Historical Association's annual convention in San Francisco, December, 1983, entitled "Political Corruption in the Young Republic."

54. "Memorandum Book of A. Jackson commencing April 1829," in Jackson Papers, LC.

55. I use the word advisedly. Jackson had no plan as such. His mind did not work that way, at least not in the realm of political philosophy. But what follows are the threads of his ideas that can be found in his letters, state papers, and especially the columns of the Washington *Globe*, all of which reflected his thinking without any deviation whatsoever.

56. Richardson (comp.), *Messages and Papers of the Presidents*, II, 1011–12.

class of bureaucrats that had always controlled it.[57] Whether this is true can be debated.[58] Still, at the time the perception of what had taken place during Jackson's tenure clearly held that a massive exodus of incumbent officeholders had occurred and that their places had been filled by political hacks and mindless partisans. As one man said, "The government, formerly served by the *elite* of the nation is now served, to a very considerable extent, by its refuse." The very fact that Jackson's policy became widely known as a "spoils system" reinforced the perception that the *"elite"* (however defined) had been replaced by the "masses." The furor over rotation—particularly after Senator William L. Marcy's injudicious remark "To the victor belong the spoils of the enemy," pronounced on the Senate floor—only publicized and popularized Jackson's contention that "no man has any more intrinsic right to official state than another." Henceforth, government office would be open to all —political hack or no. Even at its very worst "the spoils system" aided in the development of a government that was ever responsive to the changing results of the ballot box.[59]

As Jackson matured, his views on holding office became even more democratic. He reasoned from the premise that all offices —whether appointed or elected—must fall under the absolute control of the people. And elected offices must be filled *directly* by the people—not indirectly, as was then widely practiced. No office was excluded. In keeping with this principle, on several occasions he proposed a constitutional amendment to abolish the College of Electors in the selection of the president. "To the people belongs the right of electing their Chief Magistrate," he declared. "Let us, then . . . amend our system" so that the "fair expression of the will of the majority" will determine who serves as president. Not only would Jackson get rid of what he called all "intermediate agencies," such as the electoral college, but he would also limit the president's service to a single term of

57. See Sidney H. Aronson, *Status and Kinship in the Higher Civil Service: Standards of Selection in the Administrations of John Adams, Thomas Jefferson, and Andrew Jackson* (Cambridge, Mass., 1964), *passim*.
58. A fine review of the various opinions among scholars about Jackson's handling of the patronage is William F. Mugleston, "Andrew Jackson and the Spoils System: An Historiographical Survey," *Mid-America*, LIX (1977), 113–25.
59. Parton, *Jackson*, III, 220; Richardson (comp.), *Messages and Papers of the Presidents*, II, 1011.

either four or six years. He advocated a single term in order to place the president "beyond the reach of any improper influences . . . and [so] that the securities for this independence may be rendered as strong as the nature of power and the weakness of its possessor will admit." In Jackson's mind, as in the minds of the Revolutionary fathers, it was the corruption of the executive that starts the process by which liberty is ultimately lost. The American Revolution began with the efforts of the king to bribe his ministers and the Parliament to serve his interests rather than the common good. Any legitimate method, therefore, that would guard the president against the corrupting influences of ambitious and greedy politicians necessarily advanced the liberties of the people.[60]

Those who hate or fear democracy, Jackson argued, believe that "the true principle of the Government [is] that the Electors should be always AT FULL LIBERTY to choose a President for the people, instead of the people choosing for themselves." But this is a "federal principle," he declared, namely "that THE CHOICE OF PRESIDENT IS NOT THE RIGHT OF THE PEOPLE UNDER A PROPER CONSTRUCTION OF THE CONSTITUTION!"[61] On the contrary, Jackson said, neither the electoral college nor the House of Representatives nor any other body has the right to defeat the people's presidential choice. Experience proves, he went on, that the more agents selected to execute the will of the people the more the people's wishes will be frustrated. "Some may be unfaithful; all are liable to err."[62] And when the election devolves on the House of Representatives, "it is obvious the will of the people may not be always ascertained, or, if ascertained, may not be regarded." This is especially true when a single representative casts the vote of his state in the House election. "May he not be tempted to name his reward?" So Jackson called for a constitutional amendment to implement his democratic scheme and suggested that the mode of election could be regulated so as to preserve to each state its present relative weight in the election.

60. Richardson (comp.), *Messages and Papers of the Presidents*, II, 1101.
61. Washington *Globe*, October 30, 1832. This newspaper is an excellent means of getting into Jackson's thinking on a wide variety of issues, as well as his ideas about government, because he and Francis P. Blair, the editor, spoke daily about what information and what opinions the journal should carry. Blair acknowledges this fact in his letter to Jackson, May 26, 1837, in Jackson Papers, LC.
62. Richardson (comp.), *Messages and Papers of the Presidents*, II, 1010.

He further suggested that representatives in Congress be disqualified as candidates, since the election might end up in the House.[63]

Not only should presidents win election through the direct action of the people, according to Jackson, but the upper house of Congress should also come under their immediate control. At that time, United States senators were elected by state legislatures. As far as Old Hickory was concerned, senators should be popularly elected, like members of the House of Representatives, and their term in office limited to four years. In his mind the Senate was an elitist body of men committed to the principles of aristocracy and totally unrepresentative of the American people. Considering his long and bitter struggle with the upper house over the Bank of the United States (among other issues), his attitude is not surprising. His thoughts on democratizing the Senate were conveyed to the electorate in the editorial columns of the Washington *Globe* at the height of the controversy over the removal of the Bank's deposits that led eventually to Jackson's censure by the upper house. "We say, then, to the People of the United States," editorialized the *Globe*, "is it not worthy of consideration to provide an amendment to the Constitution, limiting the senatorial term to four years and making the office elective by the People of the several States?"[64]

Ideally, then, Jackson would shape the federal government so that the president would be limited to six years, senators four, and representatives two; all of them would be elected directly by the people, thereby providing a more democratic system of government. Only the president would be restricted to a single term with no possibility of reelection; this would place him beyond the reach of corrupting influences that would endanger the liberties of the people. (Consider what the nation would have been spared had Richard Nixon not wasted his time and energies on engineering his reelection.) Finally, the shape of the government would be determined by appointees who would be "rotated" with the president every four or six years, depending on the length of the chief executive's term in office. In a real sense, then, the

63. *Ibid.*, 1010–11.
64. Washington *Globe*, April 1, 1834. Jackson's support of the idea can be found in several entries in his memorandum book, in Jackson Papers, LC.

people would influence the selection of virtually every member of their government. As for federal judges, Jackson also advocated their direct popular election. He would include judges of the Supreme Court once the Constitution had been properly amended. Moreover, he would limit judicial terms to seven years but permit reelection. Obviously, Jackson was so devoted to the democratic system of office holding in all areas that he could conceive of no better method of preserving freedom and ensuring justice for all. His remarkably advanced views were far more democratic than the American people could tolerate at the time. Indeed, they are unacceptable even today. The historian and politician George Bancroft interviewed Jackson on the subject and recorded some of the president's opinions. "He thinks," Bancroft wrote, "*every* officer should in his turn pass before the people, for their approval or rejection. In England the judges should have independence to protect the people against the crown," but not in America: "Here the judges should not be independent of the people, but be appointed for not more than seven years. The people would always re-elect the good judges."⁶⁵

Obviously, Jackson had a most optimistic opinion of the people as to their capacity for self-rule. He considered them virtuous and politically intelligent. And he firmly believed that they would always act wisely.

In advancing his concept of democracy, Jackson capped all these suggestions and possible constitutional amendments with a doctrine he called "the right of instruction." This doctrine evolved from a number of basic Jacksonian principles rooted in the belief that freedom is best preserved by adhering strictly to majority rule. Opponents of the doctrine, declared the *Globe*, contend that "man is not capable of self-government and that the theory of a Republic where men will be equal is founded in error and can never be reduced to successful practice."⁶⁶ The doctrine of instruction argued that because the people were indeed capable of self-government, that because they were virtuous and wise, and that because the government had been established to serve their interests and needs, it necessarily followed that the people had the right to instruct their

65. Manuscript Ledger, in Bancroft Papers.
66. Washington *Globe*, August 21, 1835, commenting on a statement of the American Manufacturers of Pennsylvania, which is reprinted.

representatives on how they should vote with respect to particular issues. Indeed, the New Jersey General Assembly in the fall session of 1835 placed these principles on the record in the form of a series of resolutions. "The people of New Jersey," read the first resolution, "feel that the General Government . . . was formed for them . . . the PEOPLE." Therefore, "whereas in all representative governments, the sovereignty of the People is an indisputable truth, they have the right, and it is their duty, upon all proper occasions, to instruct their representatives in the duties which they require them to perform." This resolution preceded a statement directing New Jersey's senators in Congress to expunge the censure of Jackson passed by the upper house during the previous session because he had removed the government's deposits from the Bank of the United States over their objections.

Jackson himself believed very strongly in the right of instruction and on several occasions congratulated those representatives who abided by it. Indeed, he said, the only way to distinguish true Democrats from "Whigs, nullies & blue light federalists" is to ask them whether they "subscribe to the republican rule that the people are the sovereign power, the officers their agents & representatives, and they are bound to obey or resign."[67] The demand that representatives resign if they could not or would not obey the command of their constituents developed considerably during the Bank War, and in fact it happened that several senators did resign rather than submit to dictation on the issue of the removal of the deposits or the censure resolution.[68]

Naturally, there were many objections to this Jacksonian principle, mainly the contention that representatives must act as their independent consciences dictate. They must not be pressured. They must be guided only by their concern, as they perceive it, for the community at large. Another argument against the right of instruction claimed that a representative does not represent simply his own district but rather the entire country and therefore he may sometimes have to act in opposi-

67. Jackson to Donelson, May 12, 1835, in Donelson Papers. During the War of 1812 "blue light federalists" were believed to have signaled British ships off the New England coast with blue lights to indicate a save haven.
68. Senator John Tyler of Virginia, for example, resigned rather than heed the instructions of his state concerning the removal of the government's deposits.

tion to the good of his district to advance the welfare of the nation. The public good must not yield to the special interests of any portion of the Republic, argued these critics. It was also contended that a binding instruction "impedes the work of national legislation" in that it deprives the entire country of the benefits and advantages that grow out of the debates in Congress. If legislators must vote the expressed will of their constituents, then what is the use or purpose of debating issues? Representatives would simply become rubber stamps, and the task in Washington would consist merely of recording the votes dictated to them by the electorate. Finally, it was argued that the people at home can never be as good judges of what best serves the larger community as the men in Congress, who have access to more and better information and to the collective wisdom of those in attendance. The people are in fact disqualified, insisted one opponent of the doctrine, because given their education and habits, they cannot form a just estimate of public measures. That is the very reason they commit public measures to "wiser heads."[69]

The response by Democrats to this latter argument speaks directly to what the Jacksonians meant by democracy: They answered that taken individually, each citizen no doubt is inferior in learning and intelligence to his representatives in Congress. But taken collectively, the sum total of the citizenry's "intelligence and discrimination" is vastly superior to any representative or to any group of representatives, whatever may be the latter's attainments.[70]

Under normal circumstances, the Jacksonians contended, representatives should and will be left alone to vote independently. If the public does not like the general effect or results of their performance, they will remove them at the next election. It is only when the public reacts strongly to an issue, enough to make its will known through some appropriate channel, like the legislature or a state convention, that representatives in Congress *must* obey.

Thus, Jackson's legacy with respect to the question of democracy is something quite specific that was rather advanced

69. The debate over this issue can best be followed in the public prints during the latter half of Jackson's second administration. See, for example, the Washington *Globe* and the *National Intelligencer* for 1834, 1835, and 1836.
70. Washington *Globe*, January 21, 1835.

(if not impractical) for its time. It is not some vague notion about the rise of the common man or the increase of social mobility around the country—these were really the inventions of historians at a later time. And it is certainly not rhetorical mummery or claptrap—this idea is another invention of historians. Rather it is the firm and unwavering belief that the operation of government must always reflect the majority will. Many of Jackson's specific proposals, such as the abolition of the electoral college, a single term for the president, and the election of federal judges, failed to find general approval and probably never will. (It should be remembered it took nearly one hundred years to achieve the direct election of United States senators!) It can be imagined what the American experiment might have become if Jackson's other precepts had been followed: namely, if all officials of the government came regularly and directly before the people for their approval and if periodically they were rotated back home.

The intensity of Jackson's call for greater democracy throughout the operation of the American system of government, his desire for reform and economy to root out corruption and inefficiency by the Washington bureaucracy—however feeble and ineffective the results—and his belief and trust in the people, which he trumpeted at every occasion, account in large measure for the democratic surge of the 1830s and help explain why the term *democracy* replaced *republicanism* in American discourse. Jackson and his friends suggested standards to which the American government can continue to aspire when committed to the doctrine that the majority governs this nation. But it begins with a Jeffersonian faith in the great masses of people. "Our government," Jackson reiterated many times, "is founded upon the intelligence of the people. . . . I for one do not despair of the republic; I have great confidence in the virtue of the great majority of the people."[71]

What is so extraordinary about Jackson's legacy is the degree to which it has appealed not only to the most liberal Americans but also to the most conservative.[72] And it still appeals to these disparate groups; for Jackson's ideological creed contains

71. Jackson to James Hamilton, Jr., June 29, 1828, in Bassett (ed.), *Correspondence of Jackson*, III, 412.
72. This point is nicely developed by Harry L. Watson in his article "Old Hickory's Democracy," *Wilson Quarterly* (Autumn, 1985), 132.

strong elements characteristic of both of the two opposing sides of the political spectrum. Both rest naturally and comfortably with Jackson and his followers. The seeming contradictions and inconsistencies in the Jacksonians' philosophy were not so much the efforts of master politicians to appeal to any and all sides of the major issues—although skeptical historians prefer to think of them that way—as they were the effort to maintain the best of republicanism and yet adjust to the realities of an emerging industrial age.

The contradictions and ambivalences begin with Jackson himself. Not only did his personality run to polar extremes—his cruelty, violence, and rage were as much a part of his character as his gallantry, gentleness, and kindness—but his entire life as well as his political ideology included conflicting contrasts. A poor orphan boy with little appreciable education, he rose to hold the first office in the land and die a man of considerable wealth. Without military training or knowledge, he won the greatest military victory for American arms up to that time. A slave owner all his adult life, he regarded liberty as the priceless heritage of all men. A staunch advocate of equality, he thought only in terms of white adult males. Women, blacks, and Indians did not enter his thinking about liberty or equality, and his public statements to Congress invariably included the most racist ideas prevalent at the time. Jackson came into office with a promise that he would reform the bureaucracy and restore morality to government; yet his administration was charged with deepening the corruption of government through a "spoils system" that rewarded political hacks at the expense of able administrators. Despite warnings from Martin Van Buren, the president appointed Samuel G. Swartwout the collector of the Port of New York, and Swartwout has the dubious distinction of being the first man in American history to steal a million dollars from the United States Treasury.[73] Thus, Jackson, who constantly intoned the need for virtue and morality, set the stage for machine politics and boss rule. Partisanship, patronage, and the shenanigans of political ballyhoo marked the advent of Jacksonian Democracy.

It should also be repeated that Jackson failed totally to institute any substantive democratic changes in the formal republi-

73. Niven, *Van Buren*, 450–51, 474–75.

can structure of the government, despite his repeated requests to the Congress. The election of presidents by the College of Electors, the election of senators by state legislatures, and the appointment of judges for life all survived the "onslaught" of Jacksonian Democracy.

Furthermore, in the matter of the popular will, Jackson tended to see himself as the embodiment of that will—no one else. He genuinely believed that the people wanted what he had decided was best for them. His overwhelming popularity and victories at the polls reinforced this perception, and he therefore took great exception to anyone who disagreed with or contradicted him. It was almost impossible for him to conceive that someone else might have the competence to define the popular will. When he insisted that Congress and the courts obey the will of the majority, he translated that to mean that they must obey *him*. Some historians, therefore, have argued that Jackson's so-called "democratic ideology" was merely a rationalization designed to allow him to do as he pleased. But Jackson was correct in presenting himself as "the representative of all the people." No other public figure remotely approached him in popularity. And like any good politician, he told himself that when the people elected him, they did so because they believed in what he preached and wanted it practiced in their government.

Another thing: with all Jackson's talk about equality and liberty and democracy, his fundamental political philosophy was grounded in the most conservative views of his day. He advocated limited government. He believed that a strong central government endangered liberty and that therefore it was essential to keep government at the weakest level consistent with the needs of running the country. The masthead of his party newspaper carried the slogan: THE WORLD IS GOVERNED TOO MUCH. Furthermore, he preached economy in government as another prerequisite for the preservation of liberty. The American farmer and worker should be left free to enjoy the fruits of their labors and not be burdened with taxes that only swell the bureaucracy and encourage the government into unwarranted areas of activity. Thus, debt reduction constituted a cardinal doctrine of Jackson's political faith. The elimination of the national debt was something he determined to achieve during his administration, and it afforded him enormous satisfaction when he attained his goal in 1835.[74]

The notion that the government by its actions might produce a "monied aristocracy" led to another basic Jacksonian tenet, namely that the government must never play favorites, must never grant special privileges or advantages or monopolies to particular groups. The government must serve as "honest broker" among all classes of society; otherwise it could easily create a monied aristocracy that would "ultimately destroy the liberty of our country." That was one reason why he vetoed the rechartering of the Second Bank of the United States. It was what equality was all about. Equal protection under the law meant that everyone could enjoy the full benefits of his individual labor. It did not mean the equal distribution of wealth. As he said in his Bank veto message, the government must refrain from enacting laws that "make the rich richer and the potent more powerful."[75]

The very basis of "the great radical principle of freedom," said Jackson, rested on "equality among the people in the rights conferred by the Government."[76] Whatever the government does must be done equally to all. Special privileges cannot be enacted; those already enacted must be repealed.

Since freedom, according to Jackson, rested on equality, then it was essential that majority rule form the basis of government. Any other mode necessarily tilted government in favor of "the predatory portion of the community." Equality of suffrage, extended to all white males twenty-one and over, presumably ensured against legislative, executive, or judicial favoritism. It never entered Jackson's thinking that the suffrage might be extended to other races and the other sex. Thus, majoritarianism, in his view, provided the greatest safeguard for equality and, as a consequence, guaranteed the preservation of freedom.

The kind of democracy that Andrew Jackson advocated reflected his desire to buttress the society he knew, a society in which republican virtues of simplicity, public morality, and

74. See Remini, *Jackson and the Course of American Democracy*, 222ff.
75. Richardson (comp.), *Messages and Papers of the Presidents*, II, 1153.
76. Jackson to Tilghman A. Howard, August 20, 1833, in Jackson Papers, LC.

concern for the common good permeated the thinking and behavior of the electorate and their representatives. At the start of his second administration, Jackson told Tilghman A. Howard: "If I can restore to our institutions their primitive simplicity and purity, can only succeed in banishing those extraneous corrupting influences which tend to fasten monopoly and aristocracy on the constitution and to make the Government an engine of oppression to the people instead of the agent of their will, I may then look back to the honors conferred upon me, with feelings of just pride—with the consciousness that they have not been bestowed altogether in vain."[77]

What is truly remarkable about Jackson and the legacy he left to the American people is its broad appeal—even today. It speaks to conservatives, liberals, indeed to those of almost every stripe of the political spectrum. Balancing its reverence for equality, democracy, and freedom, the Jacksonian ideology also preaches limited government, economy, support of the states in all their rights and prerogatives, and opposition to public works as a matter of principle. These dogmas constitute the very heart of conservative thinking. Liberals, of course, are attracted to Jackson's genuine belief in democracy, his insistence that the people are sovereign and rule this country through their free exercise of the suffrage. Because his war against the Bank of the United States was rooted in a moral position of opposition to the efforts of the greedy rich to rob the working poor, the liberal element in American society in each succeeding generation has been compulsively drawn to the Jacksonian reform tradition. Even radicals—especially radicals!—have been and continue to be captivated by the Jacksonian rhetoric. The struggle of the poor to protect themselves from the "predatory portion of the community," as expressed so often by Jackson and his followers in language such as that of the Bank veto message, will undoubtedly continue to appeal to radical thinkers for generations to come. Among many such expressions of Jackson's contempt for the "money predators" in society is his letter to Francis P. Blair written on June 5, 1837. "You know I hate the paper system," he wrote, "and believe all Banks to be corruptly administered, there whole object to

77. *Ibid.*

make money and like the Aristocratic Merchants if money can be made alls well, regardless of the injury to the people or the Government."[78]

The specific proposals of the Jacksonian program, such as opposition to internal improvements, revision of the tariff, bank reform, and removal of the Indians, have for the most part long since passed into history. Indeed, many historians fault the Jacksonian program as totally negative in purpose and objective. What remains viable, however, despite this criticism, is the spirit of its egalitarianism, its commitment to democratic rule, to the notion that the people acting together are somehow wise and good and virtuous and that their will is the ultimate sovereignty. The language of Jacksonian Democracy has also been faulted. It has been described as vague and ambiguous. But that surely constitutes part of its appeal and strength. For the legacy that Jackson left can cut across parties and sections and even classes and speak to individuals with a directness and persuasion that no other American political ideology can match. It offers an optimistic view of the people's capacity to govern themselves, a nostalgic reverence for past criteria of public virtue, and an insistence on the preservation of individual liberty by a close scrutiny of government and all its works. The Jacksonians were not as concerned with economic development or the advancement of a capitalist state as they are sometimes accused of having been.[79] Many of them hated paper money and the credit system and tended to regard society as nothing more than an aggregation of small property owners. Many of them distinctly opposed and feared a corporate economy. Put another way, the Jacksonians always kept one eye peeled for the threat of corporate power to democracy and a corresponding eye alert for the threat of centralized governmental power.

What Jackson and his supporters did accomplish in a positive vein, however, should not be forgotten. They provided a stirring and eloquent defense of popular government and the means by which it could be realized. As one historian has written, "The Jacksonian linkage of progressive methods and nos-

78. Jackson to Francis P. Blair, June 5, 1837, in Jackson Papers, LC.
79. See Richard Hofstadter, *The American Political Tradition and the Men Who Made It* (New York, 1948) and Bray Hammond, *Banks and Politics in America from the Revolution to the Civil War* (Princeton, 1957) for example.

talgic objectives would both plague and inspire his admirers long after his Presidency."[80] But most important, it has been the inspiration for much of the dynamic and dramatic events of the past 150 years that have shaped modern American democracy. Jacksonianism has appealed to populists, progressives, New Dealers, and all manner of reformers who care about equality and liberty. Jackson himself has rightly been credited with setting the framework — at least psychologically — for all national action that succeeded him.[81] That is a legacy few presidents or statesmen can rival. That is a legacy most Americans ought to cherish alongside the other priceless gifts won for them by the makers of this nation.

80. Watson, "Old Hickory's Democracy," 133.
81. *Ibid.*

II ❧ Indian Removal

Nowadays it is very difficult to speak dispassionately or objectively about Indian removal during Jackson's administration as president—especially for his biographer—because of the intense suffering sustained by a defenseless people in the execution of his policy. There is so much prejudice that it is nearly impossible to get a fair hearing. It is presumed almost immediately that any explanation of Jackson's purposes is necessarily an attempt to justify the mass killing of innocent people. It is extraordinary how many historians refuse to hear anything except that the policy of removal was a monstrous act and that Andrew Jackson deserves the universal condemnation of all civilized people. There is nothing further they wish to hear or discuss about it.

There is no question that in the manner of its execution the policy of Indian removal was a horror. And many, if not most, of the ways in which the tribes were induced to sign treaties of removal were also evil and unconscionable. Furthermore, the Indians were invariably cheated, even when the treaties were legitimately obtained. That said, it is hoped that a discussion of Jackson's legacy with respect to Indian removal can be attempted without arousing suspicion that some kind of justification of the mistreatment and slaughter of Indians is under way.

Fortunately, no one these days seriously indicts Jackson as a mad racist intent upon genocide. That he spoke publicly as a racist cannot be doubted, but it was the language current at the time, language that remained prevalent for more than 120 years. For the most part, Americans of the Jacksonian era tended to look upon Indians as uncivilized and their life-styles as inimical to the pursuit of intellectual, mechanical, and domestic arts. Although Jackson could be difficult and ruthless, he frequently showed great regard and respect for Indians — especially those he called "full-blooded" Indians. He was less respectful to those now referred to as mixed-bloods, whom he himself called "half-breeds." His treatment of Indians has been described as paternalistic.[1] But then he treated his soldiers in the same way — and the members of his family — to say nothing of associates and political allies. In a sense, therefore, Jackson's behavior toward Indians varied hardly at all from his behavior toward anyone else. If the tribes obeyed him and followed his instructions and commands, he acted as a kind and loving "Great Father."[2] But if they challenged him in any way, if they dared to disobey, contradict, or argue with him, he could be savage and vindictive.

There is no question that Andrew Jackson regarded the Indian as inferior to the white man. It was the same racist belief shared by most Americans at the time.[3] But Jackson's racism was somewhat less pervasive than that of his contemporaries. Although he regarded the Indian as inferior, he also believed that he could be assimilated into white society, that he could eventually become a citizen and exercise all the rights that citizens enjoyed.

Jackson's ideas about the Indians and what should be done with them were probably formulated at a very early period of his life. Upon his arrival in Tennessee from North Carolina he took part in numerous military engagements against the local "hostiles." He breathed a "great ambition for encounters with the savages," said one source, and soon found many opportunities to indulge his "passion."[4] By the time he won election as major general of the Tennessee militia and began his campaign against the Creek Indians in 1813, Jackson — or Sharp Knife, as

1. The best statement of this point, I believe, is Michael Paul Rogin, *Fathers and Children: Andrew Jackson and the Subjugation of the American Indian* (New York, 1975).
2. When historians wish to be contemptuous, they insert the word *white* into the expression, so that it reads "Great White Father." But I am not aware that the term was ever used at the time in an official way, and certainly it was not used by Jackson. As president, he simply spoke of himself as the "Great Father" and of the Indians as his "red children."
3. Easy and obvious places to find expressions of Jackson's racism are his annual messages to Congress in the sections dealing with the Indians. See J. D. Richardson (comp.), *Messages and Papers of the Presidents, 1782–1892* (Washington, D.C., 1908), II, 1000ff.
4. A. W. Putnam, *History of Middle Tennessee* (Nashville, 1859), 318.

the Indians dubbed him—had formulated an overall policy of Indian removal, although it took additional experience in negotiating with the various tribes to work out the details of the policy.[5] To start, he was determined to eliminate all potential enemies of his country from the southern frontier, and that necessitated the systematic destruction of the Indian menace in the area and the territorial expansion of the American nation into the country occupied by the so-called Five Civilized Tribes: Creeks, Cherokees, Choctaws, Chickasaws, and Seminoles. The threat of invasion from Europe into the soft underbelly of the American nation along the Gulf of Mexico could only be eliminated, to Jackson's mind, by the removal of the Indian presence in the region. His attitude was reinforced by the invasion of British troops in the War of 1812, which culminated in their defeat at Jackson's hands at New Orleans on January 8, 1815. "The lower country is of too great importance to the Union," he wrote President James Monroe in 1817, "for its safety to be jeopardized."[6]

With the ratification of the Treaty of Ghent, which ended the War of 1812, General Jackson was directed by the administration in Washington to execute Article IX of that treaty. The article stated that all possessions taken from the Indians subsequent to 1811 must be returned. Automatically that required Jackson to return approximately twenty-three million acres of land he had torn from the Creek Nation at the conclusion of the Creek War in 1814. But Sharp Knife, conscious of "national security" in the region, had no intention of returning the property, so he blithely ignored Article IX and simply continued his policy of removing the Indians from the surrendered lands. And nobody stopped him, nobody dared—not even the administration, which feared western reaction to such a move and feared rebuking a national hero (which Jackson had become on account of his victory at New Orleans) to please the British or the Indians. Moreover the administration itself approved expansion. It wanted the Indians removed.

Following the war, the Indians repeatedly challenged the invasion of their country, and the administration was com-

5. Jackson's early military career is traced in Robert V. Remini, *Andrew Jackson and the Course of American Empire, 1767–1821* (New York, 1977).
6. Andrew Jackson to James Monroe, March 4, 1817, in James Monroe Papers, New York Public Library, New York, N.Y.

pelled to appoint three commissioners to investigate and determine the limits and validity of the territorial claims of the southern tribes. Jackson was appointed one of the three, along with General David Meriwether of Georgia and Jesse Franklin of North Carolina. Naturally (and not unexpectedly) Jackson dominated the commission. In addition to their investigation the three men were expected to conclude treaties with the Cherokees, Choctaws, and Chickasaws establishing boundaries between the tribes and the American nation. By this time Jackson had certain fixed ideas about how the government should treat the Indians, and no sooner did James Monroe enter office as president on March 4, 1817, than Jackson wrote him and shared some of these ideas with him. "I have long viewed treaties with the Indians an absurdity," General Jackson began, "not to be reconciled to the principles of our Government. The Indians are the subjects of the United States, inhabiting its territory and acknowledging its sovereignty, then is it not absurd for the soverign to negotiate by the treaty with the subject." Of course it is, he went on. "I have always thought, that Congress had as much right to regulate by acts of Legislation, all Indian concerns as they had of Territories; there is only this difference, that the inhabitants of Territories, are Citizens of the United States . . . the Indians are Subjects." The Indians were entitled to the protection and "fostering care" of our nation, he continued, which should be provided by Congress. "I would therefore contend that the Legislature of the Union have the right to prescribe their bounds at pleasure, and provide for their wants and whenever the safety, interest or defence of the country should render it necessary for the Government of the United States to occupy and possess any part of the Territory, used by them for hunting, that they have the right to take it and dispose of it."[7]

This was a straightforward position. There was no confusion in it about the rights of these original settlers. Quite simply, according to Jackson, the Indians had no rights if they conflicted with the security and needs of the national government. By conquest the land belonged to the American nation. The several tribes were now subject to the authority of that nation. "The Indians live within the Territory of the United States," he

7. *Ibid.*

wrote the president, "and are subject to its sovereignty and . . . subject to its laws." If the Indians were independent and possessed "sovereignty and domain, then negotiating with them and concluding treaties, would be right and proper." But they were not independent. They were not sovereign. They were totally subject to the sovereignty of the United States. "Hence I conclude that Congress has full power, by law, to regulate all the concerns of the Indians."[8]

But why has the policy of the government, Jackson asked, pursued another direction? Why has it attempted to placate the Indians and accord them rights concerning the disposition of the land? Because of weakness, said Old Hickory, answering his own question: "The arm of Government was not sufficiently strong to enforce its regulations amongst them, it was difficult to keep them at peace, and the policy of treating with them was adopted from necessity." But now things were different, he declared. Circumstances had changed, and the government was powerful enough to enforce its laws. Moreover, the Indians could no longer hunt, because the game was gone. They must lay aside their guns and bows and arrows and "produce by labor . . . in short they must be civilized." But they would retain their "savage manners and customs," he maintained, as long as the government permitted them to roam at will over vast tracts of territory. The solution was obvious, said Jackson. The government, by act of Congress, must "circumscribe their bounds," provide agricultural tools, give protection, and "enforce obedience" to the laws passed for their benefit. The result would be immediate: "In a short time they will be civilized, and by placing near them an industrious and virtuous population you set them good examples."[9]

It is interesting to note that in 1817 Jackson would have allowed the Indians to remain in place but with the boundaries of their territories strictly circumscribed. He would still have permitted them the right to occupy land in proximity to whites.

By following his prescription for handling the Indians, Jackson wrote, more justice would be extended to them "than by

8. *Ibid.*
9. *Ibid.* Ultimately it was this policy that the government was forced to follow.

the farce" of signing treaties with them. For it was all too true, he declared, "that avarice and fear are the predominant passions that govern an Indian." Moreover, money distributed by commissioners became the instrument to corrupt a few chiefs and entice them into betraying their people. "Honor justice and humanity," Jackson concluded, "certainly require that a change of Policy should take place."[10]

Although when Jackson wrote this letter he was prepared to permit the Indians the right to remain in the territory they occupied, he was of the strong opinion that they possessed more land than they actually needed. Because their land mass was so extensive, the Indians believed they could "roam" at will. As a consequence they frequently got into trouble with whites because of their "wandering ways." The extent of their landholdings should be reduced sharply, the general declared, to the precise amount required to feed, clothe, and house the tribe. For them to possess more land than they actually needed, he continued, only fomented strife with whites, resulting in bloodshed. The way to prevent these collisions was obvious: "Their territorial boundaries must be curtailed."[11]

On September 14, 1816, after considerable haggling, the three commissioners—Jackson, Meriwether, and Franklin—signed a treaty with the Cherokees at the Chickasaw Council House. The commissioners also negotiated a treaty with the Chickasaw Nation.[12] Jackson admitted to his friend General John Coffee that the negotiations with the Cherokees had been particularly troublesome and that "we were obliged to take a firm and decided stand." Meriwether, "who is a fine old fellow," said Jackson, supported him, and their combined firmness made the difference. Remember one thing, declared Sharp Knife in instructing Coffee on the fine art of negotiating with Native Americans: "An Indian is fickle, and you will have to take the same firm stand and support it and you are sure of success." This accusation of fickleness was repeated several times in the future by other commissioners. Henry R. Schoolcraft, for example, said the same thing in 1848. "An Indian council is

10. *Ibid.*
11. *Ibid.*
12. For the specifics of these treaties see *American State Papers, Indian Affairs* (Washington, D.C., 1832–34), II, 92ff. Details of the negotiations can be followed in Remini, *Jackson and the Course of American Empire*, 327–29.

a test of diplomacy," Schoolcraft advised Commissioner William Medill concerning an upcoming treaty. "The Indians are so *fickle*, that they will change their minds twice a day. It requires some of the qualities of Job to get along with them, and their friends, the halfbreeds. But perseverance in right views will ultimately prevail."[13]

Because Jackson, like other negotiators at the time, sincerely believed that Indians were fickle and regularly changed their minds after having agreed to some proposition or treaty, he was adamant against reopening negotiations with the tribes once an agreement had been struck. For example, when the Indians demanded that negotiations be reopened because of fraud or bribery, Jackson tended to discount the charge and argue that the Indians had changed their minds for no valid reason except the hope of obtaining better terms. The Indians were frequently deceptive and treacherous, he insisted, and would argue any position on earth if they thought it would advance their interest. "Treachery of the Indian character will never justify the reposing of confidence in their profession," he declared. "Be always prepared for defence and ready to inflict exemplary punishment on the offenders when necessary."[14]

As for the charge of bribery, Jackson could not deny that it was frequently true. Indeed, he himself was guilty of it, however much he tried to explain it away or put a pleasing face on it. "It may be necessary," he freely admitted, "to make the chiefs some presents" in order to move the negotiations along. But care should always be exercised. It was essential to have proper authority for such bribes. In January, 1815, the government sent Jackson some sixty thousand dollars in goods to distribute among the tribes, and the government never did learn how he disposed of them.[15] Not that Jackson preferred bribery. He really found it demeaning. Frequently, he said, he was "compelled, not from choice, but from instructions" to offer

13. Andrew Jackson to John Coffee, September 19, 1816, in John Coffee Papers, Tennessee Historical Society, Nashville; Henry R. Schoolcraft to William Medill, September 30, 1848, in William Medill Papers, Library of Congress.
14. Andrew Jackson to Henry Atkinson, May 15, 1819, in W. Edwin Hamphill *et al.* (eds.), *The Papers of John C. Calhoun* (Columbia, S.C., 1963–), IV, 63.
15. Andrew Jackson to William H. Crawford, July 20, 1816, in *American State Papers, Indian Affairs*, II, 103; Remini, *Jackson and the Course of American Empire*, 327.

bribes. How much "more humane and just" it would be to impose federal authority over the Indians, circumscribe their territory, and provide "instruments of agriculture . . . than by corrupting their Chiefs to acquire their Country." Such methods, he said in a tone of disgust, were "inconsistent with the principles of our Government."[16]

Jackson successfully completed a treaty with the Cherokees with the help of a little bribery, which he euphemistically called "a few presents." The document was signed on September 14, 1816, and in addition to forcing the surrender of an enormous tract of Cherokee land to the south of the Tennessee River, it promised peace and friendship between the United States and the Cherokee Nation forever. Moreover, the United States granted six thousand dollars annually for ten years to the tribe and five thousand dollars to be paid sixty days after the treaty was ratified.[17]

The Chickasaws proved a bit more difficult to convince, since Jackson insisted that they cede all their land on the north and south side of the Tennessee River and down the west bank of the Tombigbee River to the Choctaw boundary in Mississippi. In effect this would provide land for white settlers from Tennessee to the Gulf of Mexico. As compensation the United States offered a grant of $12,000 per annum for ten years and $4,500 in sixty days for any improvements on the lands surrendered. When the Chickasaws resisted his blandishments, Sharp Knife again resorted to bribery, and again these "presents" convinced the chiefs to accede to his demands. It was a formidable purchase.[18]

Since these negotiations came on the heels of the War of 1812, Jackson was very conscious of the need to acquire sufficient Indian lands so that a good military road could be run

16. Jackson to John C. Calhoun, August 24, 1819, in Hamphill *et al.* (eds.), *Papers of Calhoun,* IV, 271–72; Jackson to Calhoun, August 25, 1820, in Andrew Jackson Papers, Library of Congress.

17. Jackson, David Meriwether, and Jesse Franklin to William H. Crawford, September 20, 1816, in *American State Papers, Indian Affairs,* II, 105; Grace S. Woodward, *The Cherokees* (Norman, 1963), 135; R. S. Cotterill, *The Southern Tribes: The Story of the Civilized Tribes Before Removal* (Norman, 1954), 200.

18. Arrell M. Gibson, *The Chickasaws* (Norman, 1971), 105. Terms of the treaty can be found in *American State Papers, Indian Affairs,* II, 92.

from Kentucky to the Gulf.[19] Not only would such a road provide for the defense of the nation, but it would place Spanish possessions in the area—Florida, especially—in jeopardy. Within a year he and his friend John Coffee mapped plans for such a road.[20] By 1817 it was under construction; by January, 1819, it was completed and ran 483 miles from Nashville to Lake Pontchartrain, thereby facilitating the rapid movement of troops in the Southwest and shortening mail service from New Orleans to Washington to seventeen days.[21]

Without wasting a moment, Jackson urged President Monroe to open the Chickasaw and Cherokee lands he had acquired to settlers. "Nothing can promote the wellfare of the United States," he told the acting secretary of war, George Graham, "and particularly the southwestern frontier, so much as bringing into market, at an early day, the whole of this fertile country."[22] Almost immediately, settlers poured into "this fertile country." Coffee and a number of Jackson's other Tennessee cronies invested heavily in the area, forming the Cypress Land Company and purchasing excellent land at the foot of Muscle Shoals. Jackson himself speculated in the schemes, although his motive probably had less to do with economic gain than with promoting the country's defense.

Concern for the military protection of the nation prompted Jackson, who was now in command of the southern division of the army, to pepper President Monroe with nagging calls to adopt a course of action that would permanently separate the northern from the southern tribes. Prior to the War of 1812, the great Shawnee chief Tecumseh had unsuccessfully labored to unite these tribes into one consolidated mass with which he

19. Like the Cherokees and Chickasaws, the Choctaws also agreed to a settlement when confronted by U.S. commissioners. John Coffee was one of them, and through Coffee, Jackson dominated the proceedings even though he was not present himself. See treaty with the Choctaws, in *American State Papers, Indian Affairs*, II, 95; Arthur H. De Rosier, Jr., *The Removal of the Choctaw Indians* (Knoxville, 1970), 37; and Charles J. Kappler, *Indian Affairs, Laws and Treaties* (Washington, D.C., 1892–1913), II, 137.

20. On Coffee see Gordon T. Chappell, "John Coffee: Surveyor and Land Agent," *Alabama Review*, XIV (1961), 189ff.; and "The Life and Activities of General John Coffee," *Tennessee Historical Quarterly*, I (1942), 137ff.

21. William A. Love, "General Jackson's Military Road," *Publications of the Mississippi Historical Society*, XI (1910), 402–17.

22. Jackson to George Graham, December 21, 1816, in *American State Papers, Indian Affairs*, II, 123.

hoped to drive the white man back into the sea. Had he achieved his goal, the result could have been catastrophic for the American people. In one of his letters Jackson advised the president to acquire Indian lands on the Ohio River within the state of Kentucky and on the east bank of the Mississippi River. It was essential, he said, to "consolidate our settlements" and "lessen our frontier" and thereby "cut off all intercourse between the Northern Indians, and the Chickasaws and Choctaws" and ensure the safety of American commerce on the Mississippi and Missouri rivers.[23] More and more during these years following the war Jackson was becoming obsessed with the need of removing the Indians from their lands in the proximate vicinity of white settlements near or along the major rivers of the country. And it was virtually that: an obsession.

Early in 1817 the administration authorized Jackson to "extinguish the Indian titles" made in a treaty with the Cherokees in 1806.[24] This authorization was later broadened to permit Jackson to arrange an exchange of land with the Cherokees in accordance with an agreement concluded in 1808. It seems that the Cherokees had agreed in 1808 to surrender territory on the east side of the Mississippi in return for land in Arkansas. In subsequent years several thousand Cherokees had moved to Arkansas, but they failed to cede a corresponding amount of land in the East. Jackson was now given the task of convincing the eastern Cherokees that they must provide a compensatory cession. He was also authorized to grant additional lands to those eastern Cherokees who would remove to the Arkansas River and the area immediately adjoining the Osage boundary line. Thus, for the first time Jackson became directly involved in implementing the principle of removal of Indians to the area west of the Mississippi River.[25]

Naturally, during the negotiations the Cherokees contested Jackson's version of what happened in 1808. They insisted that

23. Frank Lawrence Owsley, Jr., *Struggle for the Gulf Borderlands: The Creek War and the Battle of New Orleans, 1812–1815* (Gainesville, Fla., 1981), 11ff.; Jackson to Monroe, March 4, 1817, in Monroe Papers.
24. Graham to Jackson, January 13, 1817, in *American State Papers, Indian Affairs*, II, 140.
25. Graham to Jackson, May 16, 1817, in *American State Papers, Indian Affairs*, II, 143.

they had authorized no exchange and that those Cherokees who had moved to the Arkansas had done so on their own initiative without obligating the Cherokee Nation in any way, all of which infuriated Jackson. He accused the assembled chiefs of calling him a liar. But then he never liked to be contradicted—and certainly not by Indians. So he resorted to threats. "Look around and recollect what had happened to our brothers the Creeks," he warned. A similar fate awaited the Cherokees, he predicted, if they persisted in their "unfriendly and hostile" attitude.[26]

Cowed and intimidated, the eastern Cherokees signed the treaty prepared for them on July 8, 1817.[27] They ceded two million acres of land in Georgia, Alabama, and Tennessee and received in return an equivalent amount of land on the west side of the Mississippi with the understanding that the United States reserved the right to build military roads and posts in the area if necessary. Those who removed—approximately six thousand Cherokees over the next two years—received a rifle and ammunition, one blanket, and one brass kettle or beaver trap. In addition, the United States agreed to provide flat-bottomed boats and provisions to assist in the removal. Those who preferred to remain in the East and "who may wish to become citizens of the United States" were granted 640 acres by the government, which heads of families might hold in fee simple.[28]

By the time Jackson had completed the negotiations for this treaty, if not a few months earlier, he had definitely worked out in his mind the principal parts of his Indian policy. All of it came from other statesmen, including past presidents, starting

26. "Instructions of a Deputation of Our Warriors . . . for the Affairs of the Cherokee Nation," September 19, 1817, in *American State Papers, Indian Affairs*, II, 145. Remini, *Jackson and the Course of American Empire*, 333–35, gives details of these negotiations.

27. Jackson was not always successful in his first negotiations with Indians. He failed with the Choctaws in 1819 but succeeded the following year. Thereafter he was for a time reluctant to undertake other negotiations with the Indians, though he soon relented. De Rosier, *Removal of the Choctaw Indians*, 50–51.

28. Treaty with the Cherokees, July 8, 1817, in *American State Papers, Indian Affairs*, II, 130; Charles C. Royce, *Indian Land Cessions in the United States* (Washington, D.C., 1900), 684–85, plate 15.

with Thomas Jefferson.[29] By the summer of 1817 he was reciting it to his good friend and fellow commissioner John Coffee, and parts of it showed up in his correspondence with the secretary of war and President Monroe. Jackson believed that the steady increase and movement of the white population was slowly surrounding and pressuring the Indians into adopting one of two possible courses of action: either "to become industrious Citizens" and accept the sovereignty of the states in which they lived; or to "remove to a Country *where* they can retain their ancient customs, so dear to them, that they cannot give them up in exchange for regular society." In other words, he told John Coffee, they could stay put if they were "prepared for agricultural persuits, civil life, and a government of laws." They would become citizens of the United States, their property would be protected by law, and they would mingle with the rest of "civilized" society. But those Indians who preferred to retain "their ancient customs and habits" must remove to the Arkansas River and its environs. No other possibility existed except eventual extinction. As Return J. Meigs said to Jackson: Removal "is . . . the only measure within our power to preserve and perpetuate their existence, I mean their existence as a Distinct Community, nation, or tribe." In a short time Jackson himself began to repeat this sentiment. Removal of the Indians, he wrote, was "the only means we have in preserving them as nations, and of protecting them."[30]

In the difficult negotiations that had produced the treaties with the Indians, Jackson was naturally proud of the land mass he had acquired for the American nation. Still, he did not deceive himself about its meaning or relative significance. "The cession of land obtained is not important, but the Principle Established leads to great importance," he said. The principle was removal, that is, removal of Indians who wished to preserve their identity as Indians. Those Indians who would

29. Reginald Horsman, "American Indian Policy and the Origins of Manifest Destiny," in Francis Paul Prucha (ed.), *The Indians in American History* (New York, 1971); Wilbur R. Jacobs, *Dispossessing the American Indian* (New York, 1972); and Bernard Sheehan, *Seeds of Extinction* (Chapel Hill, 1973), give useful background information.

30. Return J. Meigs to Jackson, May 24, 1817, Jackson to Calhoun, September 2, 1820, in Jackson Papers, LC; Jackson to Coffee, July 13, 1817, in Coffee Papers; U.S. Commissioners to Graham, July 8, 1817, in *American State Papers, Indian Affairs*, II, 140–47.

become cultural white men and "who are prepared here for civill life" might remain in the East, provided they became subject to state as well as federal law. As such, the "security of all" was guaranteed by these treaties, Sharp Knife declared.[31]

General Jackson's commitment to the principle of removal resulted primarily from his concern for the integrity and safety of the American nation. It was not greed or racism that motivated him. He was not intent on genocide. Nor was he involved in a gigantic land grab for the benefit of his Tennessee cronies—or for anyone else. After living with the Indian problem for many years and experiencing any number of encounters with the various tribes, both hostile and friendly, he came to the unshakable conclusion that the only policy that benefited both peoples, white and red, was removal. The extinction of the Indian, to his mind, was inevitable unless removal was officially adopted by the American government. And the official adoption of this policy he was determined to achieve. Between 1816 and 1818, in three separate actions, he had negotiated treaties with the Chickasaws and Cherokees and had acquired an enormous domain for the American people. More important, he had steadily moved to a position of determination that the Indian tribes must either be removed beyond the Mississippi River or submit to state and national authority. By the time the government called upon him in the early fall of 1820 to conclude a treaty with the Choctaw Nation, Jackson's mind was closed on the question of Indian removal. He reminded the secretary of state, John Quincy Adams, that the nation's foreign policy must take into account the fact that "we are [presently engaged in] removing [the Indians] west of the Mississippi." Thus, when he met the Choctaws at Doak's Stand, he told them that they must remove if they wished to remain Choctaw or else "you must cultivate the earth like your white brothers. You must also, in time, become citizens of the United States, and subject to its laws."[32] The Choctaws resisted his arguments and tried unsuccessfully to reason with

31. Jackson to Coffee, July 13, 1817, in Coffee Papers; U.S. Commissioners to Graham, July 8, 1817, in *American State Papers, Indian Affairs*, II, 140–47.
32. Charles Francis Adams (ed.), *Memoirs of John Quincy Adams* (12 vols.; Philadelphia, 1874–77), IV, 238; Jackson to Calhoun, June 19, 1820, in Hamphill *et al.* (eds.), *Papers of Calhoun*, V, 196; Journal of the Convention, 1820, in Jackson Papers, LC.

him, but after Jackson threatened them—"If you refuse . . . the nation will be destroyed," he flatly warned—they reluctantly capitulated and ceded some of the finest land in the United States. It was the heart of the delta. The cession involved nearly thirteen million acres—roughly a third of their eastern domain—and the Choctaws received comparable lands in what is now the southern half of Oklahoma and part of southwestern Arkansas. A rifle, molds, wipers, and ammunition sufficient for hunting and defense for one year were provided each warrior, along with enough corn to support him and his family for a year. One interesting clause in the treaty reserved some of the ceded land to be sold at auction in order to provide funds for the support of Choctaw schools in the new territory.[33]

The Treaty of Doak's Stand, signed on October 18, 1820, was a model of Indian removal. It disposed of an "alien" people and obtained rich lands in the delta of west-central Mississippi. It is not surprising, therefore, that the state of Mississippi named its new capital after Andrew Jackson. It was a fitting tribute for his contribution to the state's growth and prosperity.

As far as Jackson was concerned, the Treaty of Doak's Stand fulfilled all his ideas about the proper policy to be followed with respect to the Indians. Thereafter it became his fixed purpose to convince the federal government that this policy must be followed whenever negotiations were undertaken to acquire Indian territory. His goal was achieved sooner than anticipated. Within a few years he found himself, as president of the United States, in the enviable position of having the authority to translate the policy and principle into concrete action.

Elected president in 1828, Jackson made Indian removal a prime concern of his administration. Because the affairs of the Indians fell under the supervision of the secretary of war, he first searched for a War Department head whose position on removal was identical with his own. Since he also wanted a personal friend in his cabinet with whom he could share confidences, Jackson combined his two desires into a single appointment by selecting his old friend and Senate colleague from Tennessee, John H. Eaton, to serve as secretary of war. Eaton

33. De Rosier, *Removal of the Choctaw Indians*, 67; Doak's Stand treaty, in *American State Papers, Indian Affairs*, II, 225. See also Kappler, *Indian Affairs*, II, 191–95; and Royce, *Land Cessions*, 700–701, plate 36.

may have presented other problems by his presence in the cabinet but not the problem of what to do with the Indians. On this question he served Jackson loyally and well. Also, the appointment of John M. Berrien of Georgia as attorney general further strengthened Jackson's hand in dealing with the Indians. Berrien, it was well known, was a firm advocate of removal.[34]

In his inaugural address, delivered on March 4, 1829, before some twenty thousand people, Jackson went out of his way to say that his administration would follow a "just and liberal policy" toward the tribes "within our limits" and "give that humane and considerate attention to their rights and their wants which is consistent with the habits of our Government and the feelings of our people." Once in office he quickly implemented his "just and liberal policy" by urging the Cherokees and Creeks to surrender the remainder of their eastern lands and move west. He seemed particularly anxious to initiate negotiations in view of recent state legislation in Georgia, Alabama, and Mississippi that claimed jurisdiction over the Indians living within state boundaries. To assist him in his efforts, Jackson sent the former governor of Tennessee, William Carroll, to Georgia to urge removal.[35] He also gave Thomas L. McKenney, former head of the Bureau of Indians Affairs and a recognized advocate of the Indian cause, the job of winning support for his policy from religious leaders around the country who held strong feelings about Indian claims and the necessity of honoring their treaty rights. It was one of Jackson's shrewdest appointments. But to no avail. No matter how much he tried in several different ways to convince the Indians to leave the East, the tribes stoutly resisted. They would not abandon "their homes and ancient haunts" in favor of some unknown wilderness out west. So Jackson warned them. If they got into a dispute with the states in which they resided, they could not expect the federal government to assist them. "The arms of this country can never be employed," he wrote, "to stay any state of this Union, from the exercise of those

34. On Jackson's cabinet appointments see Robert V. Remini, *Andrew Jackson and the Course of American Freedom, 1822–1832* (New York, 1981), 161ff.

35. Richardson (comp.), *Messages and Papers of the Presidents*, II, 1000–1001; "Instructions to General William Carroll . . . May 20, 1829," in *Senate Documents*, 21st Cong., 1st Sess., Document No. 1, serial 160.

legitimate powers which attach, and belong to their sovereign character."[36]

The discovery of gold in Georgia in areas claimed by the Cherokees heightened white demand for Indian removal, but it also complicated Jackson's efforts because it triggered a white invasion of Cherokee territory, which brought howls of protest from pro-Indian groups around the country. Under the circumstances Jackson decided to hold off any further action until Congress reconvened in December, 1829, at which time he included in his State of the Union address a long section on the Indian question. In preparing his own version of this address Jackson said, "The condition of the Indians within the limits of the U. States is of a character to awaken our sympathies." The policy of the government, he wrote, sought to open to them the ways of civilization and wean them from their "wandering habits" into a course of life calculated "to present fairer prospects of comfort and happiness." It was wrong, he asserted in a forthright statement of his personal position, to encourage the Indians to the idea of "exclusive self government. It is impracticable." The idea of a free, independent, sovereign Indian state located within the states of the Union he found incompatible with a free, strong American nation. Besides, the Indians were not ready for such an exercise in self-government. No people were ever capable of carrying into execution a social compact for themselves "until education and intelligence was first introduced." The Indians east of the Mississippi River had been told, he went on, that they could not continue their "efforts at independence within the limits of any of the states."[37]

Jackson's advisers and speech writers decided to tone down these general statements and speak more directly to the immediate problem of Georgia and Alabama. So the final printed version of his address said: "I informed the Indians inhabiting parts of Georgia and Alabama that their attempt to establish an independent government would not be countenanced by the Executive of the United States, and advised them to emigrate beyond the Mississippi or submit to the laws of those States." The fate of the Mohegan, Narragansett, Dela-

36. Ronald N. Satz, *American Indian Policy in the Jacksonian Era* (Lincoln, 1975), 14–18; Jackson to the Creek Nation, March 23, 1829, in Records of the Bureau of Indian Affairs, Record Group 75, National Archives.
37. Jackson's draft of his first message to Congress, in Jackson Papers, LC.

ware, and other "dead tribes" was fast overtaking the Cherokees, Creeks, and Choctaws. "Humanity and national honor demand that every effort should be made to avert so great a calamity," the president declared.

But what about protecting the Indians with federal power in the lands they still occupied? "It is too late" for that, Jackson insisted. "It is too late to inquire whether it was just in the United States to include them and their territory within the bounds of new States, whose limits they could control. That step can not be retraced. A State can not be dismembered by Congress or restricted in the exercise of her constitutional power."[38]

Yet the situation was not hopeless, he continued. Something could be done—and he had just the solution: removal! "I suggest for your consideration," he told the Congress, "the propriety of setting apart an ample district west of the Mississippi, and without the limits of any State or Territory now formed, to be guaranteed to the Indian tribes as long as they shall occupy it, each tribe having a distinct control over the portion designated for its use." Each tribe would be subject to no other control from the United States except what was required to maintain peace on the frontier and between tribes. The emigration would be voluntary, he said. And this was an important point with Jackson. The Indians were to decide the question themselves with no coercion. But, he declared, those who refused to emigrate were subject to the jurisdiction and laws of the states.[39]

Jackson's own party, the Democrats, controlled this Twenty-first Congress and so immediately got to work to enact the president's proposal into law. Each house referred the matter to its committee on Indian affairs, and both committees were headed by Tennesseans: John Bell in the House of Representatives, and Hugh Lawson White in the Senate. The Senate committee reported the first bill on February 22, 1830; two days later the House committee reported the second. The bills had many similar characteristics, which might have been expected given Jackson's interest and the presence of his henchmen on both committees. Both established an area west of the Missis-

38. Richardson (comp.), *Messages and Papers of the Presidents*, II, 1021.
39. *Ibid.*

sippi to be divided into enough districts to accommodate as many tribes as agreed to move, and both provided the means of removing them there. An exchange of land was also included. Both bills triggered heated debate over the constitutional and moral implications of removal, and Senator Thomas Hart Benton of Missouri said the Senate debate on the issue was one of the most contested of that session.[40]

When the Senate bill came up for debate on April 6, it touched off a donnybrook. Senator Theodore Frelinghuysen of New Jersey led the opposition and spoke for three days. A deeply religious man who genuinely cared for the Indians, he attacked what he called the hypocrisy of the administration and its Democratic cohorts in Congress. The bill actually applied to *all* Indians, not just the southern tribes, he said. Its true purpose was to achieve either total removal of the Indians or their complete abandonment to the "tender mercies" of the states. But the Indians had a right to refuse to surrender their lands, he argued. They had natural rights of ownership. They had treaty rights. To threaten or harass them only invited violence and bloodshed. He pronounced Georgia's dispute with the Cherokees a simple violation of the Indians' treaty rights. The United States, he said, was obligated to protect the Indians against all transgressors, including sovereign states.[41]

The president's intrusion into the question was noted by Frelinghuysen during the course of his remarks, and he termed it highly reprehensible. It was done, he declared, "without the slightest consultation with either House of Congress, without any opportunity for counsel or concern, discussion or deliberation, on the part of the co-ordinate branches of the Government, to despatch the whole subject in a tone and style of decisive construction of our obligations and of Indian rights." Congress must not permit this improper action to go unnoticed, he maintained. "We must firmly protest against this Executive disposition of these high interests."

Moreover, he continued, the Indians had never known anything but the white man's greed. They listened to "our profes-

40. *Register of Debates*, 21st Cong., 1st Sess., 1124–25; Joseph H. Parks, *John Bell of Tennessee* (Baton Rouge, 1950), 37; L. Paul Gresham, "The Public Career of Hugh Lawson White," *Tennessee Historical Quarterly*, III (1944), 303; Thomas Hart Benton, *Thirty Years' View* (2 vols.; New York, 1854), I, 164.
41. *Register of Debates*, 21st Cong., 1st Sess., 309–20.

sions of friendship." The whites called them brothers, and they believed it. They had already surrendered millions of acres to the needs and demands of white people, "and yet we crave more. We have crowded the tribes upon a few miserable acres of our Southern frontier: it is all that is left to them of their once boundless forests: and still, like the horse-leech, our insatiated cupidity cries, give! give! give!"[42]

Frelinghuysen's savage thrusts prompted an equally savage response from John Forsyth of Georgia. What hypocrisy, he sneered. "The Indians in New York, New England, Virginia etc etc are to be left to the tender mercies of those States, while the arm of the General Government is to be extended to protect the Choctaws, Chickasaws, Creeks and especially the Cherokees from the anticipated oppressions of Mississippi, Alabama and Georgia." What the North and East had already gotten away with was now to be denied the South, he said. Robert Adams of Mississippi took up where Forsyth left off. Anyone living within the boundaries of a particular state, he contended, was subject to the laws of that state, and that included Indians. Otherwise chaos would result. Or was there now another set of rights? he asked. In addition to federal and states' rights, would there now be "Indian rights"?

Senator Peleg Sprague of Maine took a different tack in arguing against the bill. He reminded the Senate of its responsibility to carry out the terms of the treaties already signed with the Indians. Protection had been "solemnly promised," he said, and the government could provide nothing less. Ascher Robbins of Rhode Island agreed with Sprague and added his opinion that White's bill was unconstitutional. "If these Indian nations are competent to make treaties, then this proposed law . . . is unconstitutional" for the simple reason that it assigned the treating-making power to Congress while the Constitution said it was the prerogative of the president and the Senate.[43]

A number of senators, following the lead of David Barton of Missouri, asked for an amendment guaranteeing that there would be open negotiations with the Indians and that threats and other forms of intimidation would not be used to force the Indians into signing treaties of removal. But this was rejected. Frelinghuysen also offered an amendment to delay removal

42. *Ibid.*
43. *Ibid.*, 325, 359–69, 345, 354, 357, 377.

until Congress could determine whether the western lands were adequate for the needs of the Indians. Again, it was rejected. The Jacksonian majority would tolerate no alteration of their chief's proposal. So on April 26, 1830, the bill came up for a vote and passed the Senate by the count of 28 to 19. The vote followed strict party lines.[44]

If Jackson's Indian policy took a pounding in the Senate, it was nearly annihilated in the House. Indeed, the bill came within an ace of defeat. When the Senate bill arrived in the House, John Bell's own removal bill had not yet come up for debate. Bell's committee therefore let the Senate bill take precedence. Debate began on May 13 and continued for two weeks. Although the Democrats held a majority in the House, they lacked strong leadership and discipline. Moreover, many of them feared reprisals from certain religious groups within their constituencies, such as the Quakers, if they voted for removal. They knew they might jeopardize their own political future.

Debate in the House opened with a powerful salvo from Henry R. Storrs of New York, who accused Jackson of attempting to overthrow the constitutional authority of the states as well as assume the right to abrogate existing treaties with the Indians. "If these encroachments of the Executive Department," he said, "are not met and repelled in these halls, they will be resisted nowhere. The only power which stands between the Executive and the States is Congress. The States may destroy the Union themselves by open force, but the concentration of power in the hands of the Executive leads to despotism, which is worse. Of the two evils, I should prefer the nullifying power in the States—it is less dangerous."[45]

Wilson Lumpkin of Georgia dismissed the arguments against the bill as simply an expression of party politics. Most of its present opponents, he said, had supported a similar plan under the Adams administration. The intention of the bill, as everyone knew, was the preservation of Indian life. Removal was "their only hope of salvation," and that was clearly the president's wish and intention. "No man entertains kinder feelings toward the Indians than Andrew Jackson," he declared.[46]

44. *Ibid.*, 383. See also Satz, *American Indian Policy*, 25.
45. *Register of Debates*, 21st Cong., 1st Sess., 1002.
46. *Ibid.*, 1021–24.

But William Ellsworth of Connecticut brought up a point that was potentially devastating to an administration that wished to be frugal and had committed itself to a policy of limited federal expenditures. The cost of removal, said Ellsworth, might run into the millions: "We are first to purchase the country they leave, then to remove them, to conquer or purchase the country assigned them, and after this to sustain and defend them for all future time. How many millions will this cost?" Ellsworth therefore said he opposed the bill and begged the House "not to stain the page of our history with national shame, cruelty, and perfidy."[47]

By this time it had become clear that one of the great concerns of the House was the fact that General Andrew Jackson was the man in charge of removal. In the minds of some, Sharp Knife was a barbarian who could kill Indians without batting an eye. Maybe Lumpkin believed the president had kinder feelings toward the tribes than most, but some congressmen had grave doubts. So it was suggested in the course of the debate that an independent commission be appointed to administer removal and not leave it exclusively to the president. Even supposedly loyal Democrats felt uncomfortable about blindly following the president. For example, Joseph Hemphill of Pennsylvania knew how unpopular removal had become among his constituents, and so he proposed a substitute bill in which removal would be postponed for a year in order to dispatch a commission to gather information about the land to which the Indians would be sent. By delaying action, he said, Congress would thereby accept responsibility for removal and then could intelligently decide the manner in which to implement it, so that the president could be directed in the appropriate ways to execute the law.[48]

Delay seemed just the thing. It was an escape from a terrible dilemma, especially among Democrats who dreaded having to face either the wrath of their president or the wrath of their constituents. So when the vote on Hemphill's substitute measure was called, a large number of Democrats supported it. A tie vote resulted: 98 in favor, 98 opposed. It took the vote of Speaker Andrew Stevenson of Virginia, a loyal party man, to

47. *Ibid.*, 1030.
48. *Ibid.*, 1132–33.

kill Hemphill's substitution. At this juncture the president himself felt that he had better step in if he expected to save the bill. He applied considerable pressure on the House Democrats and told them that he "staked the success of his administration upon this measure." As a result, the bill narrowly squeezed through on the final vote by the count of 102 to 97. Martin Van Buren said that of Pennsylvania's twenty-six representatives — of whom all but one were Jacksonians — only six voted for the bill. They "felt themselves constrained to shoot the pit," was the way he put it.[49]

When the slightly modified House version of the bill was returned to the Senate for approval, there were final efforts by Frelinghuysen, Sprague, and their allies to burden it with further amendments, such as one restricting the removal policy to Georgia, but they all failed. The Indian Removal Act of 1830 was approved, and Jackson signed it on May 28, 1830. This was probably the most significant piece of legislation to be passed during the early years of Jackson's administration. By it he was authorized to exchange unorganized public land beyond the Mississippi for Indian land in the East. Those Indians who moved would be given perpetual title to their new land as well as compensation for improvements on their old. The cost of their removal would be undertaken by the federal government. The Indians would be given assistance for their "support and subsistence" for the first year after removal, and an appropriation of $500,000 was authorized to implement these provisions.[50]

Of the many dire predictions and warnings voiced during these debates over the Indian removal bill that eventually came true, two deserve particular attention. The first was the promise that the Indians would not be forced to remove against their will. That high and noble sentiment, repeatedly expressed by Jackson, was forgotten in due course. Among other things bribery and deception were practiced by whites on red men to drive them from their homeland. It is a sad and shameful history. The second prediction involved the cost of the operation. Congress had appropriated $500,000, but the actual

49. Remini, *Jackson and the Course of American Freedom*, 263; John C. Fitzpatrick (ed.), *Autobiography of Martin Van Buren* (Washington, D.C., 1920), 289.
50. U.S. *Statutes*, IV, 411–12.

cost was incalculable in view of the resulting bloodshed and deaths incurred by removal. In purely material terms something like 100 million acres of Indian land was added to the public domain at a cost of roughly $68 million and 32 million acres of land west of the Mississippi River.[51]

Jackson was extremely anxious to implement the Indian Removal Act, and so he tried to win treaties from the principal southern tribes as quickly as possible. He and Secretary of War Eaton invited them to attend a meeting to discuss what action should be taken. By and large the Indians ignored the invitation, but the president's personal intervention demonstrated that he meant to initiate removal immediately. At length the Choctaws agreed to meet Jackson's commissioners on September 15, 1830, at Dancing Rabbit Creek in Noxubee County, Mississippi. The terms of removal were announced by the commissioners, and these terms formed the basis of the final treaty signed on September 27 and 28. According to the Treaty of Dancing Rabbit Creek the Choctaws agreed to evacuate all their land in Mississippi and emigrate to an area west of the Arkansas Territory in what is now Oklahoma. The Indians would receive money, household and farm equipment, subsistence for one year, and reimbursement for improvements on their vacated property. They ceded 10.5 million acres of land east of the Mississippi River. They promised to emigrate in stages: the first group in the fall of 1831, the second in 1832, and the last in 1833.[52]

The Treaty of Dancing Rabbit Creek was the first removal treaty under President Jackson to win Senate approval. The action by the Senate occurred on February 25, 1831, by the vote of 35 to 12. Unfortunately, the actual removal was delayed until late fall and produced avoidable horrors that resulted in many Choctaw deaths. The entire operation was marked by inefficiency, confusion, stupidity, and criminal disregard of the rights of the Indians. It typified all too accurately the agony of Indian removal during the entire Jacksonian era.

Certainly the administration never intended to inflict such torment and outrage upon these helpless people. But good

51. Satz, *American Indian Policy*, 97.
52. Details of these negotiations can be traced in Remini, *Jackson and the Course of American Freedom*, II, 270ff.; Royce, *Land Cessions*, 726; De Rosier, *Removal of Choctaw Indians*, 122, 128; Kappler, *Indian Affairs*, II, 221–27.

intentions did not save lives. Since Jackson genuinely believed
that the Indians must be removed or "disappear and be forgotten," he hurried the process as much as possible, probably more
than was wise.[53] Far more supervision and control could have
(and should have) been provided by the administration to
guarantee the protection of Indian life and culture. But Jackson
lost his concern for the welfare of the tribes as he became more
and more obsessed with their removal.[54] The constant arguing
against his policy only hardened his determination to carry it
out—at all costs.

In October, 1832—a year and a half after the Choctaw treaty
was ratified—the Chickasaws capitulated and signed an allot-
ment treaty to complement their earlier acceptance of the
inevitability of removal. They had given their consent to
remove on August 31, 1830, prior to the Choctaw exodus, provided they received an agreeable home in the West.[55]

Jackson was less fortunate in arranging immediate removal
with the other southern tribes. The Cherokees and Creeks opted
to sue in the courts and placed themselves in the hands of William Wirt, a former United States attorney general. Their action
truly annoyed the president. "We leave them to themselves, and
to the protection of their friend Mr. Wirt," the general growled,
"to whom they have given a large fee to protect them in their
rights as an independent Nation; and when they find that they
cannot live under the laws of Alabama, they must find, at their
own expence . . . a country, and a home." As for Wirt, said
Jackson, "he had been truly wicked" and will surely bring about
"the distruction of the poor ignorant Indians."[56]

The Cherokees proved particularly difficult. Under the guid-
ance of Wirt and his associates, they filed suit in the Supreme
Court for an injunction to force Georgia to respect their rights.
In the case *Cherokee Nation* v. *Georgia*, Wirt argued that the
Cherokees had a right to self-government as a foreign nation
and that this right had long been recognized by the United
States in its treaties with the Indians. He hoped to show that

53. Remini, *Jackson and the Course of American Freedom*, 275.
54. Some indication of this obsession can be seen in Jackson's letter to Coffee, November 6, 1832, in Coffee Papers.
55. Remini, *Jackson and the Course of American Freedom*, 271, 275.
56. Jackson to William B. Lewis, August 31, 1830, in Jackson-Lewis Papers,
New York Public Library, New York, N.Y.; John Henry Eaton to John Donelly,
August 11, 1830, in Jackson Papers, LC.

Jackson himself was guilty of nullifying federal law, an argument he knew must have an impact on Marshall. In effect he challenged Jackson's entire removal policy by asking for a restraining order against Georgia.[57]

Chief Justice John Marshall handed down the decision of the Court on March 18, 1831. He rejected Wirt's argument that the Cherokees were a sovereign nation. He also rejected Jackson's contention that they were subject to state law. The Indians, the chief justice said, were "domestic dependent nations," subject to the United States as a ward to a guardian. They were not subject to individual states, he declared. Indian territory was in fact part of the United States.[58]

Quite naturally, the Cherokees chose to regard the opinion as essentially favorable in that it seemed to command the United States to protect their rights and property. So they refused to submit to Georgia law and Georgia sovereignty. Meanwhile, Georgia enacted legislation in late December, 1830, prohibiting white men from entering Indian territory after March 1, 1831, without a license from the state. This law was clearly aimed at troublesome missionaries who encouraged the Indians in their intransigence. Samuel A. Worcester and Dr. Elizur Butler, two missionaries, defied the law and were arrested and sentenced to four years' imprisonment in a state penitentiary. Nine other missionaries were apprehended but accepted pardons from the governor in exchange for a promise that they would cease violating Georgia law. Worcester and Butler rejected the condition of the pardon and were remanded to jail. They sued for their freedom, and in the case *Worcester* v. *Georgia* the Supreme Court declared on March 3, 1832, that the Georgia law was unconstitutional. Speaking for the majority, Marshall added that all the laws of Georgia dealing with the Cherokees were unconstitutional. He issued a formal mandate two days later ordering the Georgia superior court to reverse its decision.[59] The Court then adjourned.

Previously, Georgia had refused to acknowledge the Supreme Court's right to direct its actions and had boycotted the judicial proceedings. Thus, the state had no intention of obeying the

57. The report of the Cherokee suit against Georgia can be found in 5 *Peters* 1ff.

58. *Ibid.*, 15–20.

59. 6 *Peters* 515.

Court's order, whatever it might be. Since the Court had adjourned without doing anything but declare Georgia law invalid, there was nothing further for the federal government to do to implement the decision. Not until the Court either summoned state officials before it for contempt or issued a writ of habeas corpus for the release of the two missionaries could any further action be taken by the government. President Jackson was therefore under no obligation to act. According to the Judiciary Act of 1789 the Supreme Court could issue an order of compliance only when a case had already been remanded without response; and since the Court had adjourned and would not reconvene until January, 1833, action in the case ceased.[60] Not only was the president under no obligation to act, but there was some question as to whether the Court itself could act, since the existing habeas corpus law did not apply in this case because the missionaries were being detained by state authorities, not federal authorities. And since the Superior Court of Georgia did not acknowledge in writing its refusal to obey, Marshall's decision hung suspended in time. It was lifeless at the moment. Jackson understood this. He knew there was nothing for him to do. "The decision of the supreme court has fell still born," he wrote John Coffee, "and they find that it cannot coerce Georgia to yield to its mandate."[61]

Horace Greeley later reported that Jackson's response on hearing the decision was total defiance: "Well: John Marshall has made his decision: *now let him enforce it!*"[62] Greeley mentioned George N. Briggs, a representative from Massachusetts, as his source for the statement. The quotation certainly sounds like Jackson—there is no mistake about that. But the fact is that Jackson most probably did not say it, because there was no reason for him to do so. There was nothing for him to enforce. The decision was "stillborn." Why, then, would he refuse an action that no one asked him or expected him to take?

60. Edwin Miles, "After John Marshall's Decision: *Worcester* v. *Georgia* and the Nullification Crisis," *Journal of Southern History*, XXXIX (1973), 527.

61. Jackson to Coffee, April 7, 1832, in Coffee Papers.

62. Horace Greeley, *The American Conflict: A History of the Great Rebellion in the United States of America, 1860–'64* (2 vols.; Hartford, Conn., 1865), I, 106.

Even though Jackson probably did not use the exact words Greeley put in his mouth and even though no direct action was required at the moment, most historians have argued that the quotation represents in fact Jackson's true attitude. There is evidence that he "sportively said in private conversation" that if—and the "if" must be emphasized—summoned "to support the decree of the Court he will call on those who have brought about the decision to enforce it."[63] Actually nobody—including the two missionaries—expected Jackson to enforce anything, and therefore a lot of people simply assumed that the president would defy the Court if pressured. Historians have been a little too quick in faulting Jackson for something he did not do or say, and they thereby miss an important point. What needs to be remembered is that the president reacted with extreme caution to this crisis because a precipitous act could have triggered a confrontation with Georgia at the same time that South Carolina was challenging federal authority. Prudence, not defiance, best characterized his reaction to the challenge of Georgia. As one historian has said, Jackson deserves praise for his caution in dealing with a potentially explosive issue and should not be condemned for his so-called inaction.[64]

Still, Old Hickory had encouraged Georgia in her intransigence. He was so desperate to achieve Indian removal—the obsession again—that he almost produced a crisis between federal and state authorities. Nor can it be denied, as one congressman noted, that "Gen Jackson could by a nod of the head or a crook of the finger induce Georgia to submit to the law."[65] Obviously, Jackson chose not to nod his head or crook his finger. His reasons were several, the most important of which was his determination to remove the Cherokees. Moreover, as the time neared for the Supreme Court to reconvene and deliberate on Georgia's defiance, the controversy with South Carolina over nullification intensified. Jackson had to be extremely cautious that no action of his induced Georgia to join South

63. Charles J. Johnson to [?], March 23, 1832, in David Campbell Papers, Duke University Library, Durham, N.C.

64. Richard P. Longaker, "Andrew Jackson and the Judiciary," *Political Science Quarterly*, LXXI (1956), 350.

65. Lewis Williams to William Lenoir, April 9, 1832, in Miles, "After John Marshall's Decision," 533 n. 32.

Carolina in the dispute.[66] Nullification might lead to secession and civil war. Again, he acted with extreme caution. He carefully maneuvered to isolate South Carolina at the same time he forced Georgia to back away from its position of confrontation. He needed to entice Georgia into obeying the court order and freeing the two missionaries. Consequently he moved swiftly to win removal of the Indians. Through his secretary of war he quietly convinced the legal counsel for the missionaries and friends of the Cherokees in Congress that he would not budge from his position to remain aloof from the operation of Georgia laws. He convinced them that the best solution for everyone was for the Indians to remove. Although Senator Theodore Frelinghuysen "prayed to God" that Georgia would peacefully acquiesce in the decision of the Supreme Court, he soon concluded that the Cherokees must yield. Even Justice John McLean, who wrote a concurring opinion in the *Worcester* case, counseled the Cherokee delegation in Washington to sign a removal treaty.[67] Simultaneously, Jackson wrote to Lumpkin, urging him to avoid providing the Supreme Court with a "legal jurisdiction" to intervene further. He also worked through mutual friends to talk the governor into pardoning the missionaries. Finally, when Wirt agreed to make no further motion before the Supreme Court and the missionaries petitioned the governor for their freedom, Lumpkin capitulated and on January 14, 1833, ordered Worcester and Butler released from prison.[68] The danger of confrontation passed, and the removal of the Indians began in earnest.

When the *Worcester* decision was handed down, John Ridge, the astute, educated, and politically ambitious son of Major Ridge, one of the wealthiest leaders of the Cherokees and the Speaker of the Cherokee National Council, recognized imme-

66. On the Nullification Controversy see Robert V. Remini, *Andrew Jackson and the Course of American Democracy, 1833–1845* (New York, 1984), 8–44; and William W. Freehling, *Prelude to Civil War: The Nullification Movement in South Carolina, 1816–1836* (New York, 1966).

67. Miles, "After John Marshall's Decision," 530.

68. Jackson to Lumpkin, June 22, 1832, in Jackson Papers, LC; Martin Van Buren to Jackson, December 22, 1832, in Martin Van Buren Papers, Library of Congress; Benjamin F. Butler to Wilson Lumpkin, December 17, 1832, in Gratz Collection, Historical Society of Pennsylvania, Philadelphia; Marvin R. Cain, "William Wirt Against Andrew Jackson: Reflection of an Era," *Mid-America*, XLVII (1965), 113ff.

diately that the high court had rendered an opinion that abandoned the Indians to their inevitable fate.[69] He happened to be in Washington at the time and therefore went to see President Jackson and asked him directly whether the power of the United States would be exerted to execute the decision and force Georgia's compliance. The president responded in unmistakable terms that it would not.

Under the circumstances he advised Ridge "most earnestly" to go home and tell his people that their only hope of relief was in abandoning their country and removing west of the Mississippi River. Ridge left the president, reported Amos Kendall, "with the melancholy conviction that he had been told the truth. From that moment he was convinced, that the only alternative to save his people from moral and physical death, was to make the best terms they could with the government and remove out of the limits of the states. This conviction he did not fail to make known to his friends; and hence rose the 'Treaty Party.' "[70]

Ridge returned home to his family, "whom he found exulting in the decision of the Supreme Court." He woefully told them that their hopes were utterly delusive. The only prospects of Cherokee liberty lay in removing to the West; their nationality in the East was forever extinguished. They had no alternative but to follow the path that a "cruel destiny pointed out to them."[71]

The emergence of the Treaty party, mentioned in Kendall's letter, and led by Major Ridge, John Ridge, Elias Boudinot, the editor of the *Cherokee Phoenix*, and Boudinot's brother, Stand Watie, among others, resulted in efforts by these leaders to get the best treaty possible with the United States. They accepted the reality of Jackson's determination to remove them, and so they set about the business of relocating. But the Treaty party was a minority faction of the Cherokee Nation. Most Cherokees opposed removal and formed the "National party" under the leadership of Principal Chief John Ross, the charismatic, tough, proud, and determined son of an immigrant Scot and a mixed-blood mother. His manner, appearance, and life-style were white, but he considered himself an Indian, and Jackson

69. Jackson to Coffee, April 7, 1822, in Coffee Papers.
70. Amos Kendall to William L. Marcy, November, 1845, in Amos Kendall Papers, Library of Congress.
71. *Ibid.*

agreed—a very bad Indian, the president said, "a great villain."[72] The president detested the Principal Chief because of Ross's active and successful efforts to block his removal plans. Moreover, Jackson honestly believed that Ross headed a mixed-blood elite intent on centralizing tribal power and revenue for their own economic self-interest. It was the same sort of thing he encountered in his own society. Ross and his followers, according to the president, were the Indian equivalents of the pro-Bank aristocrats in the United States. "Real Indians," Old Hickory sneered, wanted no part of this modern Cherokee state that aimed only at satisfying the corrupt values of mixed-bloods. "Real Indians," like the Ridges, acknowledged Jackson's deep concern for the welfare of his "red children" and understood that further resistance to his policy would surely result in the ultimate annihilation of the Cherokee Nation.[73]

Jackson had still another reason for disliking and distrusting Ross. According to the president, Ross "often proposed to make a treaty for mony alone & not Land." Moreover, he would "let the Cherokees seek their own country beyond the limits of the United States—to which," continued Old Hickory, "I always replied we were bound by treaty to keep our Indians within our own limits."[74] (This proprietary concern for "our Indians" was typical of Jackson.) Quite simply, then, the president regarded the Principal Chief as nothing but a greedy little "half-breed" who cared nothing for the moral or material interests of his people.

So Jackson refused to deal with the Principal Chief and directed his negotiating team to deal solely with the Treaty party. But this attitude was quite improper because—like it or not—Ross was the Principal Chief and spoke for the majority of Cherokees. The Reverend John F. Schermerhorn, an ambitious cleric who had been helpful in obtaining a removal treaty with the Seminoles, spearheaded Jackson's drive to force the Cherokees into agreeing by treaty to removal. All of which

72. Jackson to Van Buren, October 5, 1839, in Van Buren Papers.
73. Fragment of a memorandum in Jackson's handwriting, n.d., Jackson Papers, LC; Washington *Globe*, June 3, 1834. See also Mary Young's two Carroll Lectures entitled "Friends of the Indian," delivered at Mary Baldwin College, October 8–9, 1980 (copy in author's possession), 6ff., and also her "Indian Removal and the Attack on Tribal Autonomy: The Cherokee Case," in John K. Mahon (ed.), *Indians of the Southwest* (Gainesville, Fla., 1975), 125–34.
74. Jackson to Van Buren, October 5, 1839, in Van Buren Papers.

drove Ross to near fury because Jackson would not deal with the duly constituted authority of the Cherokee Nation as established under the Cherokee Constitution of 1827. But Jackson denied that a duly constituted authority of the Cherokee Nation existed. The Cherokee Constitution called for an election in 1832, and it had not been held. Instead, the Principal Chief filled positions on the National Council with his friends. Once more the president saw this as a fraud by elitists who disregarded the interests of the majority of their people.[75]

A draft removal treaty was quickly arranged with a minimum of difficulty and signed on March 14, 1835, by Schermerhorn and others, acting on behalf of the United States, and John Ridge, Elias Boudinot, and a delegation of Cherokees.[76] The treaty provided that the Cherokee Nation cede and relinquish to the United States its rights and titles "to all lands owned, claimed and possessed by the Cherokees, including lands reserved for a school fund, east of the Mississippi River," in return for which they would receive a sum in the amount of five million dollars. In effect, the treaty acquired from the Cherokees nearly eight million acres of land in western North Carolina, northern Georgia, northeastern Alabama, and eastern Tennessee. A program of removal was also provided, according to which the Cherokees would be resettled in the West; they would receive scheduled payments for subsistence, claims, and spoliations, and would be issued blankets, kettles, rifles, and the like. After due promulgation, the treaty was to be submitted to the Cherokee National Council for its approval and to the president for approval with the advice and consent of the Senate.

Schermerhorn, familiar with Jackson's methods of dealing with the Indians and aware that he must immediately bring the Cherokees to terms or lose the president's confidence, called "a council of all the people" to meet with him at New Echota in Georgia during the third week in December, 1835. He arranged to have a large contingent of the Treaty party present. Furthermore, he warned those who stayed away that their

75. Remini, *Jackson and the Course of American Democracy*, 294, 300. On Ross, see Rachel C. Eaton, *John Ross and the Cherokee Indians* (Menasha, Wis., 1914), and Gary E. Moulton, *John Ross, Cherokee Chief* (Athens, 1978).

76. For provisions of the draft treaty, see *House Documents*, 23rd Cong., 2nd Sess., No. 292.

absence would signify consent to whatever transpired at New Echota.

Virtually the entire Cherokee Nation stayed away, encouraged by the warnings and threats of the Principal Chief. But the Treaty party attended. On December 28 what came to be called the Treaty of New Echota—it basically repeated the provisions of the draft treaty approved in March—was approved by those in attendance at the council meeting. The vote was 79 to 7. This incredibly low number represented the merest fraction of the Cherokee Nation, certainly not the elected government of the Cherokees and certainly not the thousands of Indians who should have participated in the ratifying process if this, in fact, was "a council of all the people."[77]

The Cherokees were stunned and outraged. The ratifying process was fraudulent, no question about it. But both Jackson and Schermerhorn insisted on its legality, inasmuch as the Indians had been warned that their absence would be counted as consent to whatever was agreed upon at the meeting. The Cherokees had a choice. In electing to turn their backs on the "council of all the people," they forfeited their right to protest. For his part, Ross protested with all his many skills. A meeting of the National Council was called at Red Clay in January, 1836, and although the temperature fell below freezing and smallpox ravaged one Cherokee district, nevertheless approximately 400 persons appeared at the meeting. Some detainees sent in proxies with friends and neighbors. The council promptly passed a resolution denouncing the New Echota treaty and declaring it null and void. Eventually more than 12,000 Cherokees signed the resolution, which was forwarded to the United States Senate. Ross followed up this petition with another one, signed by 3,250 Cherokees living in North Carolina, and this, too, was delivered to the Congress.[78]

Jackson dismissed these signed resolutions just as he dismissed the petitions for the recharter of the Bank of the United

77. *Senate Documents*, 24th Cong., 1st Sess., No. 120; Charles C. Royce, "Cherokee Nation of Indians," in Bureau of American Ethnology, *Fifth Annual Report* (1887), Part 2, p. 281; Major Ridge *et al.* to Jackson, December 1, 1835, in Records of the U.S. Senate: Executive Messages Relating to Indian Relations, 1829–49, Record Group 46, National Archives; Moulton, *John Ross*, 70ff.

78. Mary Young in "Friends of the Indian," II, 26, calculated that $^{15}/_{16}$ of the entire Cherokee Nation opposed the treaty.

States. Neither the Bank petitions nor the Cherokee resolutions represented the will of the constituents, he declared. As for the Cherokees, a council had been called to represent "all the people" according to their "ancient customs." None were excluded. Why, then, had so many of them stayed away when the government offered to pay subsistence to all who would attend? The reason was obvious to Jackson: because the Principal Chief and his "half-breed" henchmen warned the Cherokees to stay away under pain of physical violence and the Indians dared not oppose his will. What reinforced Jackson's contention was the fact that the Treaty party kept assuring him that "a majority of the people" of the Cherokee Nation gratefully *approved* the New Echota treaty "and all are willing peaceably to yield to the treaty and abide by it."[79]

Another fact prejudiced the president against Ross. When the New Echota treaty was brought to Washington, the Treaty party begged the Principal Chief to join them either in support of the treaty as written or upon such alterations as would make it acceptable—given the indisputable fact that Jackson was determined to remove the Cherokees or die in the effort. "But to their appeal, [Ross] returned no answer," reported Amos Kendall.[80]

Despite Ross's heroic efforts to defeat the treaty in the Senate, it got through—but just barely. Over the mighty vocal appeals by Henry Clay, Daniel Webster, Edward Everett, and others to kill the fraudulent beast, the treaty won the required two-thirds majority. On May 18, 1836, a total of 31 senators voted for it, 15 against. The president immediately added his signature and proclaimed the Treaty of New Echota in force on May 23, 1836.[81]

Strangely, the debate over ratification in the Senate did not begin to compare with the verbal brawl unleashed by the debate over the removal bill in 1830. It did not produce a sense of moral outrage on the part of the religious community in the country. As a matter of fact, the American Board of Commissioners for Foreign Missions, whose purpose was the "civilizing" and Christianizing of the Indians, failed to support any

79. Major Ridge and John Ridge to Jackson, June 30, 1836, in Records of the Bureau of Indian Affairs, RG 75, NA.
80. Kendall to Marcy, November, 1845, in Kendall Papers.
81. Remini, *Jackson and the Course of American Democracy*, 301.

effort to defeat the treaty's ratification. The board was more concerned with winning War Department approval to set up new missions among the Osage and Chippewa tribes. Again, the Cherokees were simply abandoned to the fate Jackson had decreed for them.

Ross reacted to Jackson's arrogance in the same way Nicholas Biddle reacted when he heard about the president's Bank veto. Said Ross: "We will not recognize the forgery palmed off upon the world as a treaty by a knot of unauthorized individuals, nor stir one step with reference to that false paper." The treaty gave the Cherokees two years to prepare themselves to leave their homeland, and Ross's response was to advise his people to ignore it and remain where they were. Not everyone listened to him, however. Some two thousand Indians resigned themselves and headed west. The remainder huddled around Ross, waiting to see what would happen.[82]

The worst possible fate awaited them. When the deadline for the evacuation of all eastern Cherokees was reached—even though Jackson was no longer president and had been replaced in the White House by his handpicked successor, Martin Van Buren—the government ordered the commencement of removal. The Cherokees still resisted, and so they were rounded up, herded into prison camps, and then hurled westward along the unspeakable "Trail of Tears."

The Cherokee people need not have endured this agony. Jackson and Ross are both responsible for permitting the worst horrors of removal to occur. And they should have been prevented. Jackson was obsessive about removing the southern tribes—and that included the Cherokees, civilized or not. He badgered President Van Buren about enforcing the treaty and warned that Ross would make every effort to get it rescinded. Van Buren reassured him that nothing would slow the exodus of the Cherokees and that the two-year grace period would not be extended under any circumstances.[83]

But Ross shares blame for the tragedy. His continued defiance even after the deadline for removal passed placed his

82. Young, "Friends of the Indian," II, 26; Moulton, *John Ross*, 72–74; Mary Young, "The Cherokee Nation: Mirror of the Republic," *American Quarterly*, XXXIII (1981), 505.
83. Van Buren to Jackson, June 17, 1838, Jackson to Van Buren, July 8, 1838, in Van Buren Papers.

people in great jeopardy. Despite every sign to the contrary, he seemed to think he could frustrate the presidential will to expel the Cherokees from their land.

In all the horrors and stupidities that followed the wretched Cherokees on their trek westward, perhaps one of the most incredible has been totally overlooked. The Treaty party cooperated in the removal, and immediately after the treaty was ratified, many of them headed west, where they joined the western Cherokees or "Old Settlers," as they were called, who had preceded them many years before. The Old Settlers welcomed the Treaty party and united with them. But instead of working with the Treaty party in the removal process, said Amos Kendall, the United States "with an apparent indifference to the fate of their friends seldom unsurpassed, gave strength and power to their mortal enemy, John Ross, by putting into his hands on the most extravagant terms the entire business of emigrating the body of the nation." In the fall and winter of 1837–1838 Ross and his leaders at the heads of their clans arrived in Cherokee Country West "with a profusion of money which the government had placed in their hands. . . . Now commenced the troubles of the Old Settlers and the Treaty party. The Old Settlers were willing to receive the Ross party as they had done the Treaty party and unite with them. . . . But Ross was unwilling to part with power for a moment. He insisted that the government of the western Cherokees be abolished and a new one [formed] which of course would be controlled by him through his subservient majority." When the Old Settlers and the Treaty party refused this demand, some of Ross's friends resorted to violence. Major Ridge was ambushed and shot to death. Elias Boudinot and John Ridge were slain with knives and tomahawks in the presence of their families and friends. Thus, the effort to unite the eastern and western Cherokees, said Kendall, "was struck down by men who had opposed that policy from first to last. . . . Yes and the United States in placing the immigration money in the hands of these men gave them strength and power to persecute and murder their friends! . . . You can not appreciate the degree of censure which attaches to this government," declared Kendall, "for abandoning a party which was faithful to the United States and the true interests of the Cherokee people without a true understanding of the character of those men, or rather *that man* [John Ross], to whom they have been sacrificed." Stupid! That was the only way to describe the policy of the American government in this matter, concluded Kendall.[84] And the Cherokee people paid dearly for it.

But the Cherokees survived the torments imposed on them. As Jackson had predicted, they not only survived — they endured. Although the Cherokee Nation West lost its national domain and jurisdiction, Cherokee people today have a tribal identity, a living language, and at least three governmental bodies: the Cherokee Nation East, the Cherokee Nation West, and the Original Cherokee Community of Oklahoma. "That's more than you say of the Yemassee," concludes Mary Young.[85] It is also more than you can say for the Mohegans, Narragansetts, Pequots, Delawares, and any number of other "dead tribes."

Jackson's relentless determination to remove the Indians was applied to other tribes besides the Cherokees — and sometimes without the benefit of a treaty. The Creeks, for example, were subdued in the so-called Creek War of 1836 and forced to remove. They had resisted the frauds practiced on them by "unprincipled and wicked contractors." And for their efforts the government carted off 1,600 Indians to the West, some of them handcuffed and in chains. No treaty for this removal was ever signed.[86]

An even worse agony for both the Indians and their white tormentors accompanied the removal of the Seminoles in Florida. Jackson's efforts to hurry the process exploded in a series of bloody encounters that marked the beginning of the Second Seminole War in late 1835. Before the Indians were defeated and shipped to the West, the fighting resulted in the deaths of 1,500 regular soldiers out of 10,000 who participated, and it cost ten million dollars. There is no way to calculate the mortality among volunteer soldiers or among Indians. The war lasted until 1842.[87]

84. Kendall to Marcy, November, 1845, in Kendall Papers.
85. Mary Young, "Pagans, Converts, and Backsliders, All: A Secular View of the Metaphysics of Indian-White Relations," p. 7. I am grateful to Professor Young for permission to quote from this as yet unpublished article.
86. *Senate Documents*, 27th Cong., 3rd Sess., No. 219, p. 86; Michael D. Green, *The Politics of Indian Removal: Creek Government and Society in Crisis* (Lincoln, 1982), 174–86.
87. On the Seminole War see John K. Mahon, *History of the Second Seminole War, 1835–1842* (Gainesville, Fla., 1967).

By the close of Jackson's two terms in office approximately 45,690 Indians had been relocated beyond the Mississippi River. According to the Indian Office, only about 9,000 Indians, mostly in the Old Northwest and New York, were without treaty stipulations requiring their removal when Jackson left office. And the operation provided an empire for the United States. Something like one hundred million acres of land was acquired for approximately sixty-eight million dollars plus thirty-two million acres of western land.[88]

Jackson's legacy to the nation in terms of the removal of the Indians has brought him and the nation scathing denunciation in recent years. In his own day Americans saw his policy as a convenient means of obliterating the presence of the Indian in "civilized" society and seizing his land. Like Jackson, they defended removal as the sole means of preserving Indian life and culture. What they did, therefore, they chose to regard as humanitarian. They could assume a moral stance at the same time they stripped the Indian of his inheritance.

And both the Jacksonians and their opponents shared this conceit. Although the Whigs pummeled the Democrats for their unconscionable theft of Indian property and inhuman disregard of Indian life and safety, nevertheless they pursued Jackson's identical policy when they themselves came into office and had the opportunity of reversing or halting that policy. President William Henry Harrison not only favored Indian removal, but he chose John Bell of Tennessee, an author of the removal bill, as his secretary of war. President John Tyler followed suit. As one historian has pointed out, the Whig party found Indian removal a wonderful political weapon with which to bludgeon Democrats when the Whigs were out of power and struggling to take over the government, but when they achieved power themselves, they turned their backs on the stricken Indian and simply continued Jackson's policy without pause.[89]

It is both a happy (many tribes have survived) and a most unhappy (but at what cost) legacy. Some men, like Jackson, meant removal as a humanitarian means of preserving Native American life and culture in a place where they would not con-

88. Remini, *Jackson and the Course of American Democracy*, 314.
89. Satz, *American Indian Policy*, 53.

stitute a threat to the safety of the Union and a bother to the greed, arrogance, and racism of whites. Most Americans were delighted to be rid of the problem and still believed that they had been true to their Christian ideals and humanitarian instincts. No doubt the Indians did in fact have to be removed. No other policy was possible if they were to survive.[90] But instead of the policy involving all those noble and idealistic principles that Americans like to believe are the stuff of their history and public policy, it was executed all too frequently by a display of their worst characteristics: their greed, their pragmatism, their intolerance with anything and anyone who hinders their prosperity and ambition for personal gain.

Jackson left office believing he had found a safe haven for thousands of Indians west of the Mississippi River. He also believed that he deserved the gratitude of both the red and white races for solving a problem that no previous president had dared to tackle. In the course of time he has received neither, even though the Five Civilized Tribes endure. Instead he has merited the severest condemnation. For Americans, Indian removal is a good reminder that the best intentions in the world can sometimes end in human misery and death. They can sometimes disgrace a nation and blacken its history.

90. On this point see Francis Paul Prucha, "Andrew Jackson's Indian Policy: A Reassessment," *Journal of American History*, LVI (1969), 527–39. A magisterial study of Indian policy for the entire course of American history is Prucha's *The Great Father: The United States Government and the American Indians* (2 vols.; Lincoln, 1984).

III ❦ Slavery

Ever since Richard Brown published his article "The Missouri Crisis, Slavery, and the Politics of Jacksonism" in the *South Atlantic Quarterly* in 1966, historians have taken what I personally believe to be a totally wrong tack on the question of slavery during the Jacksonian era. William Freehling was probably the first (and certainly the most important of the early historians) to endorse the Brown thesis. Since it dovetailed perfectly with Freehling's own idea that slavery—rather than the tariff—was the underlying issue provoking the Nullification Controversy in South Carolina, it is perfectly understandable why he championed Brown's argument that the origins of the Democratic party were rooted in the need and desire to defend and protect the South's "peculiar institution." Several other historians followed this lead, and it reached a climax, of sorts, in William J. Cooper's study *The South and the Politics of Slavery*. This work advances the thesis that slavery motivated much of the politics of the South throughout the Jacksonian era and beyond.[1]

As Andrew Jackson would undoubtedly have said had he known: "There is a conspiracy in all this." Not a conspiracy among the historians just mentioned, let me hasten to add, but a conspiracy hatched by "that arch fiend, J. Q. Adams," as Jackson sometimes referred to the sixth president of the United States.[2] It is the same sort of "conspiracy" that historians accepted for

1. Richard Brown, "The Missouri Crisis, Slavery, and the Politics of Jacksonianism," *South Atlantic Quarterly*, LXV (1966), 55–72; William Freehling, *Prelude to Civil War: The Nullification Movement in South Carolina, 1816–1836* (New York, 1966); William J. Cooper, Jr., *The South and the Politics of Slavery, 1828–1856* (Baton Rouge, 1978). See also Michael F. Holt, *The Political Crisis of the 1850s* (New York, 1978), 20–21.
2. Andrew Jackson to Sam Houston, March 15, 1844, from a private collection, copy in Jackson Papers Project, Hermitage, Tennessee.

over a hundred years concerning how and why the Tariff of Abominations won passage into law in 1828, a "conspiracy" charge conceived by John C. Calhoun. It will be recalled that Calhoun, who knew nothing about the motives guiding the men who wrote and shepherded the 1828 tariff through Congress, "revealed" in a public speech (after he had alienated himself from these men) the details of their "plot" to foist an abominable tariff upon an unsuspecting country, and "revealed," too, how southern Congressmen were "tricked" into believing that the tariff had been deliberately designed to be defeated. It took a long time to disabuse historians of this error, to convince them that Calhoun knew nothing about the strategy behind the enactment of the 1828 tariff and that when he accused Martin Van Buren of deceiving southern Congressmen he simply wished to discredit all those whom he felt had been instrumental in his political downfall.[3]

The extraordinary notion that the Democratic party was formed in the 1820s with the ostensible purpose of making it an engine for the protection of slavery was probably first conceived by John Quincy Adams! An unlikely candidate, one would think, but upon reflection, Adams as the author of this canard makes considerable sense. Samuel Flagg Bemis, the distinguished biographer of the sixth president, got the idea from Adams during his research on the biography and passed it along to Richard Brown, his graduate student, with the suggestion that he check it out. In his research Brown found in the Van Buren Papers in the Library of Congress Van Buren's remarkable letter to Thomas Ritchie written on January 13, 1827, which stated that in the past party attachments had furnished "a complete antidote" to sectional prejudices. "It was not until that defence had been broken down," Van Buren continued, "that the clamour agt Southern Influence and African Slavery could be made effectual in the North." By reviving party attachments, Van Buren said, he hoped to still that "clamour."[4]

3. See Robert V. Remini, "Martin Van Buren and the Tariff of Abominations," *American Historical Review*, LXIII (1958), 903–17. To his credit, however, it should be noted that Calhoun admitted at the time that his accusations were not based on his "own personal knowledge." Richard K. Cralle (ed.), *The Works of John C. Calhoun* (14 vols.; New York, 1854), III, 48–49.

4. A conveniently available copy of Van Buren's letter in its entirety can be found in Robert V. Remini (ed.), *The Age of Jackson* (New York, 1972), 3–7.

And with that remarkable admission by Van Buren, Brown was off and running. Soon he was followed by a large contingent of historians who found the Adams thesis entirely to their liking. It confirmed all their own judgments about the role of slavery in party and national affairs.[5]

But the Adams theory about slavery and the origins of the Democratic party is just as wrong as Calhoun's theory about the enactment of the Tariff of Abominations. Both Adams and Calhoun were anxious to fix the worst possible motives upon their enemies. Both men had been badly mistreated by the leaders of the Democratic party, and both had heavy political scores to settle. Their theories, then, should be regarded with the greatest skepticism and suspicion.

Actually Van Buren structured a new party apparatus, using Andrew Jackson as the magnet to attract support from every section and class, to force a repudiation of what he called James Monroe's "Amalgamation policy," that is, a policy that strove to obliterate parties in the name of national unity and harmony.[6] To Van Buren's mind, and the minds of many other young ideologues of the post–War of 1812 era—and Martin Van Buren was an ideologue despite his reputation as a crafty political operator—parties were essential to the proper function of government.[7] There were no independent voters in the 1820s, it will be remembered. Men belonged to parties because they were committed to particular ideologies and wished their beliefs to guide the government in its actions. Parties, therefore, were essential to healthy and free governments. Indeed, as far as Van Buren believed, political parties were the only instruments by which ideology would transcend narrow sectional interests. "We must always have party distinctions," he told Thomas Ritchie, editor of the Richmond *Enquirer*, "and the old ones are the best of which the nature of the case admits."[8] He cited at least six reasons for reviving the party

5. The details of the journey of this idea from Adams to Brown were furnished the author by Richard Brown.

6. Robert V. Remini, *Martin Van Buren and the Making of the Democratic Party* (New York, 1959), 24–29.

7. This concept is discussed in careful detail in Richard Hofstadter, *The Idea of a Party System: The Rise of Legitimate Opposition in the United States, 1780–1840* (Berkeley, 1969).

8. Martin Van Buren to Thomas Ritchie, January 13, 1827, in Martin Van Buren Papers, Library of Congress.

system, and he did not include the protection of slavery as one of them. Not until he spoke of the natural and beneficial union between the planters of the South and the plain republicans of the North did he discuss geographical divisions and how prejudices between the free and slaveholding states inevitably occur. Party attachment was an antidote for sectional prejudices, he said. Once parties had been broken down, attacks upon southern influence in the country gathered momentum. Obviously, Van Buren believed that the existence of a viable two-party system would diminish the jealousy and sectional rivalry between the North and South that had sometimes expressed itself in the "clamour" against African slavery. But that is not the same as saying that the Democratic party was formed to protect slavery or, as Brown wrote, that Van Buren's proslavery strategy was "the root principle of the whole structure of ante-bellum politics."[9]

Proof of this contention is the fact that during the presidential campaign of 1828, the campaign for Jackson around which Van Buren and others had substantially reorganized Jefferson's old Republican party, the issue of slavery was never seriously raised. In that turbulent, free-swinging, uncontrolled contest, the question of slavery was not put forward at any time by either side. This is attested to by Duff Green, close friend and associate of John C. Calhoun and editor of the United States *Telegraph*, mouthpiece of the early Jackson party in Washington. Slavery was not an issue in the campaign, he wrote. "The anti slave party in the North is dying away."[10]

Nor did the question of slavery trigger the Nullification Controversy with South Carolina in 1832. It was the tariff issue (and its concomitant, states' rights) with all the heated discussion that had surrounded it for almost ten years, that prompted the confrontation between the state and federal governments. Had the issue indeed involved slavery, however hidden, other southern states would surely have sided with South Carolina. Because the nub of the controversy involved tariff

9. Brown's article "The Missouri Crisis, Slavery, and the Politics of Jacksonianism" has been reprinted in many places. I have used Edward Pessen (ed.), *The Many-Faceted Jacksonian Era: New Interpretations* (Westport, Conn., 1977), 184.

10. Duff Green to Worden Pope, January 4, 1828, in Duff Green's Letter Book, Library of Congress.

rates, and not slavery, the other southern states refused to support South Carolina's action. Nullification was not a doctrine that appealed to them. For proof, notice the action of the other southern states when the controversy flared. The Alabama legislature pronounced nullification "unsound in theory and dangerous in practice." Georgia, locked in its own disagreement with the federal government over Indian removal, said it was "mischievous, rash and revolutionary." Mississippi lawmakers chided the South Carolinians for acting with "reckless precipitancy." And the North Carolina legislature labeled nullification "revolutionary" and "subversive."[11]

In fact there has been considerable research recently by such historians as Paul Bergeron, Harry L. Watson, and James Oakes, all of whom argue that slavery did not intrude into the politics of southern states much at all in the early 1830s. Bergeron, in two articles based on quantitative data in Tennessee, concluded that slavery never really colored Tennessee politics at the time of the Nullification Controversy. Watson, in his study of Jacksonian politics in Cumberland County, North Carolina, does not find the politics of the 1830s in that area shaped by fears concerning slavery. Rather he discovered that economic issues, as traditionally has been argued, formed the basis of most of the political discussion.[12]

What has been overlooked by modern historians in their rush to find slavery in everything under the heavens is the real and stated reason for the reorganization of the Republican party between 1825 and 1828. Van Buren and others were attempting to reaffirm a political ideology that they believed was in jeopardy on account of Monroe's "Amalgamation policy." They hoped to reassert the philosophy of Jeffersonian republicanism that preached states' rights, fiscal restraint, opposition to internal improvements, and the necessity of limiting the powers of the central government. The reassertion of this philosophy was essential, they argued, to the protection of individual liberty. To the Jacksonians, therefore, the idea of

11. *State Papers on Nullification* . . . (Boston, 1834), 201, 219–23, 230, 274.

12. Paul Bergeron, "The Nullification Controversy Revisited," *Tennessee Historical Quarterly*, XXXV (1976), 263–75, and "Tennessee's Response to the Nullification Crisis," *Journal of Southern History*, XXXIX (1973), 23–44; Harry L. Watson, *Jacksonian Politics and Community Conflict* (Baton Rouge, 1981), 198ff. See also James Oakes, *The Ruling Race: A History of American Slaveholders* (New York, 1982), 123ff.

the federal government's assuming the right to interfere with slavery in the states was simply absurd. Some even denied that state governments could interfere. "The right of property exists before society," wrote Representative William O. Goode of Virginia. "The Legislature cannot deprive a citizen of his property in his slave. It cannot abolish slavery in a State. It could not delegate to Congress a power greater than its own."[13]

Jackson's position on the question, and the position of the other leaders of the Democratic party, was quite clear and unambiguous. He held that the Constitution expressly recognized slavery in the South and made provisions about representation in Congress to accommodate that fact of life. "Has it ever been pretended," asked the Washington *Globe*, Jackson's mouthpiece after his break with Calhoun and Duff Green, "that Congress has any power to subvert the basis on which the Constitution itself was founded? Has any statesman ever suggested the idea that the general government has authority to subvert not only the rights guaranteed to individuals by the Constitution [namely their right to private property] but rights recognized as appurtenant to the state institutions, and on which their ratio of representation is made to depend?" The argument of the Jacksonians, therefore, was that the slave question had been closed by the Constitution: "There is no debatable ground left upon the subject," editorialized the *Globe*.[14]

But what about the right of Congress to legislate for the territories and the District of Columbia on such issues as slavery? That "supposed right," argued the Jacksonians, was exactly what triggered the American Revolution. The members of Congress were not chosen by the people of the territories or the District and were ignorant of their wishes and welfare. The Jacksonians drew a parallel between Congress and the British Parliament on the eve of the Revolution. Thus, if Congress enacted laws for the District or the territories, on subjects and in a form "not acceptable to the majority of the inhabitants, not consonant to their education, habits, and wishes and interests, as understood by themselves, [it] violates the first principle of sound, paternal, and just legislation." When Congress "does not

---

13. Quoted in Oakes, *The Ruling Race*, 134.
14. Washington *Globe*, May 1, July 10, 1833. See also the issue of June 10, 1833.

consult the will of the majority of the governed, the foundation stone of all correct policy," it "is guilty of the same gross oppression and tyranny which was practised by the Parliament of Great Britain towards this country before 1776."[15]

Simply put, slavery and racism were deeply embedded in Jacksonian society, as deeply as they were in the society that produced the Declaration of Independence and the Constitution.

To Jackson and his followers, therefore, the question of slavery was not something the government could address with impunity. To them it was akin to discussing the right of the government to confiscate individual property. The right to hold slaves was a basic right, as basic as liberty itself. Put baldly and badly, slaveholding was as American to these Jacksonians as capitalism, nationalism, or democracy. As James Oakes remarked in his book *The Ruling Class*, it was as natural as racism. William Cooper, in *Liberty and Slavery*, has argued that the white southern celebration of liberty *always* included the freedom to preserve black slavery. That states Jackson's own position precisely.[16]

With the rise of abolitionism during the Jacksonian era, the question of slavery could not be dismissed or lightly disregarded, however much the Democrats devotedly wished to do so. Jackson himself and many of his supporters came to regard abolitionism and its intrusion into the political arena as a conspiracy of disaffected and disappointed demagogues (John C. Calhoun and John Quincy Adams, for example) who raised it for ignominious purposes. These "malcontents" sought one of two objectives: either to disrupt the Union or to discredit democracy. In either case the Jacksonians believed that the ultimate purpose of this treachery was the destruction of the Jacksonian principle that "the majority shall govern this nation." Once the principle collapsed, a republican form of government in which a minority would rule could be restored. And that minority would surely take the form of an aristocracy of money.

In all of the recent discussion among historians about slavery and its impact and influences, insufficient attention has been given to the validity of Jackson's admittedly simplistic view

15. *Ibid.*, July 28, 1835.
16. Oakes, *The Ruling Class*, 135ff.; William J. Cooper, Jr., *Liberty and Slavery* (New York, 1983).

about the motives of those intent on ending slavery. Historians have been more inclined to condemn Jackson and his followers as slave owners and racists whose only thought was the protection of their property and political interests. The entire Democratic party is seen as the creation of men whose principal object was the protection of the "peculiar institution." But like Jackson's view, this one, too, is grossly simplistic.

The Jackson position on the slavery question deserves a more careful analysis. The question of the degree of truth contained in his beliefs also needs to be explored.

It should be mentioned at the outset that like Thomas Jefferson, whose republican ideology he professed to follow, Andrew Jackson was a slave owner most of his life, bought and sold them like any other planter, treated them with savage cruelty or paternal affection (depending on circumstances), believed they were innately inferior, and did not free a single one (he owned 150 or thereabouts) when he died, although he told them he hoped to meet them all in heaven.

Then, at the conclusion of the Nullification Controversy with South Carolina, President Jackson and other leaders of the Democratic party became visibly worried about slavery as a political issue.[17] Indeed, Old Hickory rightly predicted that the next attempt to assault the Union would occur over the question of slavery. "The next pretext," he warned in a letter written on May 1, 1833, "will be the negro, or slavery question."[18] Thus, when Calhoun, James Hamilton, Jr., George McDuffie, and the other "conspirators" failed to array the South against the government over the tariff question and possibly pitch the nation into civil war, Calhoun "put his partisans upon a new tack," according to Jackson. "The slave question," announced the *Globe* on May 1, 1833, "is that which they now propose to produce commotion. Out of this they hope they will brew a storm which will unsettle all the Institutions of the country. . . . Now they seek to start a controversy in which there can be no compromise." Because the

17. I have dealt with the Nullification Controversy at some length in my Jackson biography. See Robert V. Remini, *Andrew Jackson and the Course of American Democracy, 1833–1845* (New York, 1984), 8–44.

18. Andrew Jackson to Reverend Andrew J. Crawford, May 1, 1833, Jackson to John Coffee, April 9, 1833, in John Spencer Bassett (ed.), *Correspondence of Andrew Jackson* (6 vols., Washington, D.C., 1926–33), V, 70, 56.

tariff question had failed them and because the president threatened to hang them as traitors, "it was necessary . . . for the nullifiers to make all possible haste to get their necks out of this noose and to set up some other standard of opposition" to disrupt the Union. Through their presses throughout the South and in Washington, men like Calhoun, Hamilton, McDuffie, and Robert Y. Hayne "counterfeited new-born terrors about dangers, about the security of their slave property." The *United States Telegraph* had openly broached the doctrine, declared Frank Blair, editor of the *Globe*, that the "Government of the majority" could not be borne because of the irreconcilable differences that existed between the slaveholding and nonslaveholding states. And this introduction of the slavery issue had been picked up in the North among some of Henry Clay's friends. Redwood Fisher, editor of the New York *Advocate*, for example, "again plays into the hands of the nullifiers . . . in the same spirit of collusion . . . in the new game got up in relation to the slave question." No sooner did Fisher get his signal from the *Telegraph*, claimed Blair, than he responded with the following statement: "It shall not be our fault if ever the value of free labor is reduced down to that of the slave." And again: "The tariff will not be dead though every slaveholding state in the Union shall unite to reduce the labor of free men to the level of that of slaves." Fisher's statement was the text, said Blair, that was being reechoed from all the newspapers of the nullifiers in the South, and the *Telegraph* went one step further: "Let a convention say to Congress that if you take one step toward emancipating our slaves we will simultaneously secede from the Union and form a confederacy of our own." So, declared Jackson's mouthpiece, measures would be adopted by a general convention of southern states that would force Congress to leave slavery alone.

Blair responded to the idea of such a convention in a sharply worded editorial that left no doubt of the Jacksonian position. Whenever did Congress, or any member of Congress, he snorted, propose the abolition of slavery by the authority of that body? "The Constitution of the United States expressly recognizes the slaves of the south." Neither Fisher nor any other editor north of the Potomac had even hinted that Congress would ever be asked to exercise such "usurped authority"; it was only the imaginary conspiracy created by Calhoun's press that was conjured up as a pretext for convoking a "southern convention against slavery."[19]

Although the abolitionist movement had long since been under way, it is interesting and important to note that Jackson and his spokesman regarded the introduction of the slavery question as a political issue in Congress as having been conceived by nullifiers to advance their efforts at disrupting the Union. The position of the Jacksonians in 1833, therefore, was simply this: slavery was protected by the Constitution; only those intent on mischief seriously proposed that Congress could abolish slavery; and only nullifiers like Calhoun and his friends argued that there were irreconcilable differences between slave and nonslaveholding states, for the simple reason that they hoped eventually to establish a southern confederacy.

The fact that the Jacksonians noted that some of Henry Clay's friends, like Redwood Fisher, had focused on the slavery question was not surprising. In view of the alliance between Calhoun and Clay during the Nullification Controversy[20] and continuing thereafter during the removal of the government's deposits in the Bank War, the Jacksonians naturally suspected some kind of working conspiracy between the nullifiers of the South and Clay's Whig friends in the North. And whereas the nullifiers wished to disrupt the Union to create a southern confederacy, the Democrats reasoned, the Whigs hoped to discredit democracy and return the government to elitist rule. The "moneyed power" in the country hated the idea of majority rule, which had been ushered in by Jackson, and they sought any and all means by which to annihilate the concept of democratic rule in order to restore federalism with its aristocratic conceits. "The sole object of the agitators has been to make sectional parties north and south," argued the *Globe*, "to SEVER the democracy, and defeat that unity of action in support of the popular cause which can alone prevent the triumph of the coalition of federalism working for the cause of corruption—for the moneyed power seeking to command the Chief Magistracy and the

19. Washington *Globe*, May 1, 1833. For an excellent biography of Calhoun, despite its strong prejudice in favor of its subject, see Charles W. Wiltse, *John C. Calhoun* (3 vols.; Indianapolis, 1944–51).

20. A recent study of the crisis is Merrill D. Peterson, *Olive Branch and Sword—The Compromise of 1833* (Baton Rouge, 1982).

Government through the election by States in the House against the will of the majority of the people."[21]

In their efforts to reassure southerners regarding the safety of their "peculiar institution," Jacksonians continually reminded them that although northerners had banished slavery from their own borders, "they are fully aware that the manumission of the slaves of the South would operate to the injury of northern industry—of northern interest in every way." No northern legislature, they contended, would promote universal emancipation, and if there were a general revolt of slaves against their masters, there would be a perfect unanimity among the nonslaveholding states to put it down. Nullifiers knew this, Democrats contended, and it was that knowledge that emboldened them to stir up the slave question. It was the security of that knowledge that encouraged them to raise a false alarm in order to frighten thousands of southerners into their ranks. "It is for the purpose of their political intrigues," wrote Blair, "that this force is to be rallied." The South Carolina "theatricals," as he called Calhoun, Hayne, Hamilton, and McDuffie, under the guidance of their "manager," Duff Green, were seeking to frighten the southern states "into a sort of St. Domingo tragedy." They were actors —and very good ones. They made such a cry over the tariff that South Carolina came close to secession and war, even though South Carolina was the least affected by the new protective rates. That state's great staple was rice, and she exported more of it than anything else. Governor Hamilton was "buckling on his sword as a general" to cut loose from the Union and "hazard all the blessings" the Union secured, for the sake of free trade, which he believed was lost, though he was "every day growing rich by it." It should be clear to all what lay behind this subterfuge, declared Blair. "Political objects, and not pecuniary distresses have been the real cause of these lamentations, which have been so well feigned by the South Carolina orators."[22]

These "theatricals" were conspiring to produce a southern confederacy with South Carolina at its center and Virginia and North Carolina in support from one side and Georgia and Alabama in support from the other. Charleston would become the "New York of the South," with railroads running across the

21. Washington *Globe*, May 28, 1836.
22. *Ibid.*, June 11, 1833.

mountains to bring Kentucky and Tennessee into this confederacy. And of course John C. Calhoun would preside over the
whole.[23]

As part of their grand conspiracy, the "theatricals" were not
content to excite alarm among slaveholders with regard to their
property. They also sought to create an expectation among the
slaves that in the event of a rebellion they would find support in
the North instead of a determined foe ready and willing to aid in
putting down the rebellion. Jacksonians were absolutely convinced that responsible northerners would be as horrified by a
slave rebellion as southerners and would assist with every
power at their command in suppressing it. As one indication of
the use of fright tactics by the "theatricals," the Jacksonians
singled out a statement in the Richmond *Whig* declaring that
William Lloyd Garrison's *Liberator* referred to George Washington as a hypocrite, thief, and kidnapper because he held slaves,
and that Garrison went on to state that Washington "is now in
hell!" Even the anti-Jacksonian *National Intelligencer* chided the
Whig for reprinting this outrageous assault upon the first president. "With all respect for the editors of the Richmond Whig,"
said the *Intelligencer*, "we take the liberty to deprecate the use
of arguments such as this calculated unnecessarily to excite and
alarm the passions of the south." The Jacksonians repeatedly
stated that the subject of slavery was a delicate and dangerous
question—and that it was not debatable. Those newspapers in
the South, such as the *Whig*, and those newspapers in the North,
such as the Philadelphia *Inquirer*, that "prey on the subject"
were condemned as "Jesuitical" because "only organs of mischief" strive to excite the public mind about a closed subject,
and they do it "to get up *a great crisis*."[24]

A letter dated October 17, 1831, by Harrison Gray Otis,
mayor of Boston, and published in the Boston *Patriot*, got considerable attention in the Jacksonian press at this time. In the
letter Otis denied that northerners wanted to free the slaves.
He never doubted, he said, that the states were inhibited by the
Constitution from interfering with the "plantation states," as
he called them, in the management of their own "peculiar"
institutions. "The existence of slavery is a deplorable evil," he

23. *Ibid.*, June 10, 11, 1833.
24. Washington *National Intelligencer*, July 7, 1833; Washington *Globe*,
July 19, 1833.

wrote, and was known to be an evil at the time of the adoption of the Constitution. But a compact was struck, and "it is our duty and our interest," he declared, "to adhere to it." If the blacks rose in a revolt, he continued, the government would be required to suppress it; moreover, the interests of the other states would require them to assist the measures of the government. Under these circumstances, he concluded, "I am desirous of leaving the affair of emancipation of your slaves to yourselves, to time, to the Providence of God."[25]

When the *North American Review* commented in the summer of 1833 that "some persons of intelligence in Boston" seemed to be encouraging "projects" for the immediate emancipation of slaves throughout the country, the Richmond *Enquirer* called on the Boston editorial corps to verify this contention. Several editors responded immediately, saying that the number of these so-called "persons of intelligence" was extremely small and that among northerners "not one in 100 favor the immediate abolition of slavery." The *Delaware Gazette* claimed that if one traveled from Portland to Philadelphia, he would not see a single abolitionist newspaper or tract. The *Gazette* also suspected that the subject of slavery was agitated more in the South—by such men as John C. Calhoun and Duff Green—than in the North. And they agitated it not so much because they feared abolition but rather because of their desire to shake the Union.[26]

Indeed, the Jacksonians repeatedly tagged Calhoun a troublemaker motivated by a need for revenge against the leaders of the Democratic party and a monstrous ambition to create a southern confederacy with himself as the chief officer. He was seen traveling through Georgia in late August, 1833, "to preach a crusade to excite the populace over the question of slavery." He proposed, said one observer, "to give color to the suggestion that the manufacturers of the North entertained designs to emancipate the slaves." But northerners knew, this reporter continued, that the labor situation was different in the two sections of the country, "that the negro from the want of capacity and the absence of motive to acquire skill in the arts can never become a competitor with the northern manufacturer—and . . .

25. Washington *Globe*, September 5, 1833.
26. *Ibid.*, August 28, 1833.

being more capable of labor in the hot climate of the South than the whites, he will be held to employment in agriculture and rendered the producer of raw materials which will give employment to the northern manufacturer." Nothing was more apparent to the people of the North, he said, than the interest they had in maintaining slave labor in the South.[27]

The Democrats were obviously not above making racist slurs against blacks to prove their point that northern industry was not out to free the slaves. Racism, like slavery, was rooted deeply in their society. They took elaborate pains to reassure southerners of northern good will.

With respect to Calhoun's crusade, a Georgia "gentleman of respectability" gave an account of an interview that Calhoun had with General Richard G. Dunlap of Tennessee, an interview that took place in a tavern and attracted considerable interest among the patrons of the establishment. In their discussion the general told Calhoun that his "fears on the slave question are certainly not founded on any facts which will induce the belief of the interference by the Northern people."

"We must take things by their tendency," replied Calhoun in his most somber voice. In that case, replied the general, "we can not be more alarmed at the Yankees than we would be at the rest of the nation and the whole world."

Calhoun replied by reminding Dunlap of the protective tariff, the ominous drift by "Congress toward doing everything for the general masses of people," and the deadly hunger for patronage by subservient officeholders and partisans of the Democratic party. General Dunlap interrupted. The simple cure for such evils, he said, was the intelligence of the country. "The people are the only arbiters in our government," he declared, and when they were properly informed of these evils, their patriotism would eventually produce the necessary cures and correctives.

Calhoun vehemently disagreed. It was not the people who were the arbiters of our government, he insisted, but "the States, as separate and distinct communities." They were "the judges of the usurpation of the federal Government," he lectured. "The States, as States, are the principals, and the General Government nothing more than the agent."[28]

27. *Ibid.*, September 5, 1833.
28. *Ibid.*

As this anecdote illustrates, men like General Dunlap saw the nation as a democracy in which the majority decided all questions. That was the way Jackson saw it and the way he wanted his party and the rest of the country to see it, too. And that democracy, they felt, was no more a threat to slavery than it was to landowning or farming or any other capitalistic endeavor. However, those southerners guided by Calhoun's fears and philosophy dreaded the consequence of this drift toward democracy and argued that unless the states maintained their position as "arbiters in the government," slavery would eventually be abolished. To Jackson, therefore, the only people to raise the slavery issue were those who rejected the concept of democracy and demanded, for whatever reason, government by a minority.

The moral dimension of the slavery issue never entered Jackson's mind. He never for the moment questioned whether it was right for one human being to hold another in bondage. Nor did he imagine for the moment that abolitionists really cared about the black man or his welfare. All efforts, Jackson wrote in his farewell address as president, issued on March 4, 1837, "to cast odium upon the institutions of any state and all measures calculated to disturb the rights of property or the peace of any community are in direct opposition to the spirit in which the Union was formed, and must endanger its safety." Weak men, Jackson contended, will persuade themselves that their efforts at disruption are undertaken "in the cause of humanity and . . . the rights of the human race." But be not deceived, he said. "Everyone, upon sober reflection, will see that nothing but mischief can come from these improper assaults upon the feelings and rights of others."[29] Three years later, while campaigning for Van Buren's reelection in 1840, Jackson gave a speech in which he addressed the problem of abolitionism. Again he referred to the humanitarian motives of the abolitionists. Maybe they were motivated by "real philanthropy" in advocating their cause, he allowed, but the net result was "to array one section of the Union against the other. It is in this aspect that the movements of the abolitionists become fearful and portentous." They had been manipulated in a "false direc-

29. J. D. Richardson (comp.), *Messages and Papers of the Presidents, 1782–1892* (Washington, D.C., 1908), II, 1516–17.

tion," he said, by those who were intent upon the resurrection of the "doctrines of the Federal party" and cared nothing for the black man. Their influence had been channeled in such a way as to "multiply the sources of discord between the various sections of the Union." As far as Jackson was concerned, the only point worth mentioning with respect to the abolitionists was that they were being used—used politically—for an ignominious cause. Abolitionists were subverting democracy, he warned, whether they knew it or not, and that was wrong and had to be stopped. Worse, they were shattering the Union to achieve their goal. "The election of Mr. Van Buren is essential to the preservation of republican principles," Jackson insisted. If the voters cast their ballots for him, Jackson said, "your republican system is perpetuated"; but vote for William Henry Harrison, "the chosen candidate of the apostate republicans, the abolitionists, and the Hartford Convention federalists, and your constitutional liberties are perhaps gone forever, and may end like that of ancient republics."[30]

The Democrats, including Jackson, were deluding themselves about many things, the most important of which was the notion that the agitation over slavery was simply a political question gotten up by corrupt, greedy, and ambitious demagogues. It was a convenient and tidy theory, and one they very much wanted to believe.

Southerners were reassured by the Jacksonian press that northern laborers, the real democracy of the nation, stood ready to annihilate the abolition societies that had sprung up in many northern cities during Jackson's second administration. "They are resolved," said the *Globe*, "not to allow a new competition for employment to be introduced by the introduction of increased numbers of free blacks of the free States," and they would therefore oppose emancipation "to prevent the emigration of a class of persons to the free States which . . . the most *benevolent* persons are willing to endure among them." For example, Gloucester, New Jersey, was "literally overrun by

30. Nashville *Union*, October 15, 1840, copy in Jackson Papers Project, Hermitage. The speech was written with the help of Andrew J. Donelson, but the language and ideas in it can be found in a number of letters by Jackson, all written before he gave the speech. See, for example, Jackson to Andrew J. Hutchings, August 12, 1840, in Andrew J. Hutchings Papers, Days Collection, Tennessee Historical Society, Nashville, and Jackson to Andrew J. Donelson, October 8, 1840, in Andrew Jackson Donelson Papers, Library of Congress.

blacks, driven by the violence of an infuriated mob from their homes in Philadelphia." Their numbers, "previous to this influx, had become in some places troublesome—in others a burden and a nuisance. A temporary sojourn among us, considering the circumstances of the case, may be borne with—but the first indication of a permanent residence should, and we feel confident will, call forth a rigid enforcement of the statute against the admission of blacks into our boundaries."[31]

Jackson's press, especially the *Globe*, made every effort to convince their readers that the "average working man" in the North would never countenance abolition. "The working men of the non slave holding States," said Blair on May 5, 1835, "have too much intelligence to degrade their condition in life, and diminish the means of comfortable subsistence from the labors of their hands, by encouraging the schemes of abolition societies, which, if successful, would make them competitors for employment with myriads of half-famished blacks." Indeed, "I will venture to say, that there will not be found one Democrat in twenty in all these societies. The clergy of the North are anti-democratic with a very few exceptions." The Whigs, on the other hand, "would not hesitate to liberate the blacks with a view of reducing the whole laboring classes to their level . . . depriving the great mass of the people of all political rights and build up the aristocracy upon the sacrifice of the principle of free suffrage."[32]

George McDuffie was reported as insisting that the manufacturing states wished to abolish slavery to prevent a competition between free and slave labor. However, he admitted that "the *wealth* and intelligence of the northern and middle states are opposed to any direct and unconstitutional interference with our rights of property." But later he shifted his argument, placing blame for antislavery agitation not on the "wealth and intelligence" of the North but on the "poor Democracy." McDuffie reportedly said: "It is my deliberate opinion that the unbalanced democracy of the middle and some of the northern states will pass by rapid transition, through anarchy to despotism; and I am thoroughly convinced that domestic slavery, paradoxical as

31. Washington *Globe*, August 29, 1834, quoting New Jersey newspapers, including the *American Sentinel* and Woodbury *Herald*.
32. Washington *Globe*, January 28, September 17, 1835.

it may seem, is an indispensable element in an unmixed representative republic."[33]

As the abolition societies continued to grow in the 1830s and the agitation over slavery swelled, the Democratic press took notice of the physical violence that frequently accompanied the demonstrations against slavery and suggested that the agitators, like nullifiers, deliberately fomented trouble in order to endanger the Union. Indeed, in the minds of many Jacksonians, the abolitionists were linked with the nullifiers as dissatisfied troublemakers whose true goal was the annihilation of democracy through the collapse of the Union. For example, the Presbyterian synod meeting in Philadelphia in December, 1835, warned the churches against the abolitionists who were "desperate in spirit" and were endangering the integrity of the American Union "by the unchristian methods which they adopt to advance the cause of *abolition*."[34]

Thus, when many cities experienced riots (a number of which were related to the presence of blacks in the community) and society seemed to be disintegrating into something violent and dangerous, the Whig press addressed the problem head on, claiming that the cause of the disorders was the fact that the country had changed and was no longer governed by the wise and the good but rather by the unwashed masses, who had risen to power behind the popularity of an ignorant ruffian. What has brought about "the present supremacy of the Mobocracy?" asked one Whig journal. The answer was obvious: Andrew Jackson and his "demagogue adherents." They had courted the masses for over ten years. "They have classified the rich and intelligent and denounced them as aristocrats; they have caressed, soothed, and flattered the heavy class of the poor and ignorant, because *they* held the power which they wanted." They had even stirred "the jealousy which the poor feels towards the rich." The paper appealed for the truth of these statements "to the State Papers of Gen. Jackson himself; not one of which is exempt from the reproach of an artful appeal to the passions of the poor and ignorant." Small wonder, then, that mobs felt no compunction

---

33. The Washington *Globe* ran a series of articles titled "Governor McDuffie's Opinions," and these quotations were taken from the January 26, 1835, issue.
34. Washington *Globe*, December 5, 1835.

against rioting. They were encouraged by those at the very highest level of government.[35]

A great many Whigs agreed with this assessment. They had witnessed a war hero ride to power on the enthusiasms of mobs. They watched his so-called "reforms" produce a "spoils system," a Bank War, and the establishment of executive despotism. *"The Republic has degenerated into a Democracy,"* cried the Richmond *Whig*, and democracy had produced nothing but chaotic government and social unrest.[36]

Democrats tried to warn the country about the intentions and objectives of the Whigs. A danger of catastrophic proportions, they said, that might lead to civil war and disunion, had been launched. Since "every other device" had failed, said Frank Blair, "the leadership of the opposition" had unleashed the abolitionists. "Who is the great propagator of the SLAVE EXCITE-MENT, which has already produced mobs in many of the cities and villages of the North as well as the South; which . . . has driven the father, the husband, and the master, to rush beyond the laws to destroy the instigators of a servile war . . . ? It is . . . the abolition associations . . . the *devoted instrument of an opposition* which . . . [resorts to] civil commotion, when all the ordinary political firebrands have been extinguished" (italics added). Did not the public see the connection between urban violence and the antislavery agitation? "Behold ye Liberators, Emancipators, Abolitionists, the fruits of your extravagance and folly, your recklessness and your plots against the lives of your fellow man! Behold!"

Who were these abolitionists, these enemies of the Union? They were the rich, the elite, the privileged. They were the disappointed politicians who had no popular support and therefore sought influence and power through violence. They were not motivated by concern for the slave. They simply wanted to restore elitist rule—lost in the upsurge of democracy during Jackson's administration.

"Yes," cried the president's newspaper, "Democracy is the cause of all this fury on the part of the aristocratic faction." And all because "it will not suffer a minority to rule. It will maintain the rights of the People. It will not consent that the

35. Editorial reprinted in *ibid.*, August 22, 1835.
36. *Ibid.*

Government shall succumb to a Bank monopoly. It will not surrender the Constitution to factious incendiaries, and hence it is chargeable with all crimes which those enemies of the country commit." The aristocrats desired the downfall of the people, and so they sponsored havoc over the issue of slavery and hoped to sink the entire country in the abyss of civil war. Then, when they had reduced the nation to ruin, they would reestablish their oligarchic rule and make America once more a land of the rich and powerful.[37]

Edwin Croswell, editor of the Albany *Argus*, the mouthpiece of Martin Van Buren's political machine, the Albany Regency, agreed that the Whigs blamed every evil in the country on the rise of democracy. "The Tory leaders," he wrote in a letter to George Bancroft, the Jacksonian politician and writer in Massachusetts, "labor to convey the impression that the modern tendency to violence & to the disregard of the law, arises from too great an infusion of the democratic spirit, & from the character & example of the Executive. . . . It is important . . . that the public mind . . . should be disabused on the subject; & that the excesses of the day sho'd be traced to their true source,— the . . . leaders & agents, of the Tory school, in & out of Congress."[38]

In attempting to present the position of the Democratic party on slavery, the *Globe* on December 22, 1835, with Jackson's full knowledge and approval, ran an editorial stating that the "Democratic friends of the Administration in every section of the U. States—the friends of the Union and of peace everywhere, seek to sink the irritating topic into instant significance." The policy of the administration, therefore, was simply to mute the question of slavery, not advance it or protect it. And the reason for this position was obvious: the desire of the leadership of the Democratic party to safeguard the Union and the democratic strides achieved throughout the country over the past few years.

The rise of abolitionism naturally prompted the submission of petitions to Congress to halt the spread of slavery. And early in 1836 Senator John C. Calhoun introduced a motion in the Senate to refuse to receive such petitions. The Senate con-

---

37. Washington *Globe*, August 22, 1835. See also Washington *National Intelligencer*, July 27, 1835.

38. Edwin Croswell to George Bancroft, August 13, 1836, in George Bancroft Papers, Massachusetts Historical Society, Boston.

curred, but Calhoun was determined to initiate a debate on "the sacred right of petition," not for any other reason, said Jackson and his friends, than a determination to provoke discord in Congress and thereby gain political capital in South Carolina and throughout the South. Webster would love to debate the issue for the same reason, they claimed, even though he would take the other side of the question.[39] "Webster and Calhoun work in opposition for the sake of agitation," wrote Frank Blair. They both sought "to secure a control in the midst of the convulsions of the country, which they never can expect from its united and voluntary suffrages." More and more it seemed to such political observers as Jackson and Blair that only those defeated and unpopular politicians whose ambitions for the presidency had been thwarted would stoop to such desperate measures as invoking the slave question in order to "secure a control" in the midst of the havoc they had generated. Old Federalists like Webster and John Quincy Adams, together with nullifiers like Calhoun and McDuffie, pursued the same end: to produce a "southern sectional party" that would lead to the formation of "two sovereignties, to become the prizes of aristocratic intrigue and monied monopoly." These "partners . . . *in whiggery*" sought to defeat "the popular cause which alone can prevent the triumph of the coalition of federalism working for the cause of corruption—the monied power . . . against the will of the majority of the people."[40]

If, for the sake of argument, abolitionism is considered simply as a political question, without any moral or economic or other implication, then it can be understood—if not appreciated—why Democrats would regard this particular reform movement as simply a deadly thrust of bitter and frustrated Federalists and nullifiers, both repudiated by the people, both bankrupt, both having nothing to lose and everything to gain by havoc and discord.

It was noted by the Jacksonians when the question of the admission of Michigan and Arkansas into the Union came up for discussion in Congress, late in Jackson's administration, that it, too, was made to serve the destructive purpose of these

39. A new and excellent biography of Webster is Maurice Baxter, *One and Inseparable: Daniel Webster and the Union* (Cambridge, Mass., 1984).
40. Washington *Globe*, December 22, 1835.

malcontents. "It will be seen," commented one man, "that Mr. Adams and Mr. [William] Slade [of Vermont] of the abolition faction tried to press the Missouri question upon Arkansas and thus appeal to the sectional feelings of the North so as to excite the old feud which had endangered the Union. But the Democrats of the North frowned upon this factious attempt. They united with their Democratic brethren in the South to vote down all the incendiary movements. . . . Upon all the votes [on this question] the abolitionists and nullifiers were seen voting together."[41]

The question of the right of petition of course, did not disappear, and it served to provide what John Quincy Adams' biographers have agreed was his finest hour. The first petition had been presented to the House of Representatives on December 16, 1835. Representative James H. Hammond of South Carolina, one of Calhoun's messmates in Washington, moved that it not be received. Ultimately it was tabled—but not before a nasty debate that lasted six weeks had occurred. Then, in May, 1836, the House passed a resolution introduced by a committee chaired by Henry L. Pinckney of South Carolina that declared that any interference with slavery in the District of Columbia was inexpedient, and in the states unconstitutional. It also directed that all petitions, memorials, resolutions, and the like relating in any way to slavery or its abolition "be laid upon the table," without "either being printed or referred . . . and that no further action whatever shall be had thereon." The adoption of the Pinckney resolution, with its so-called gag rule, inaugurated a running battle over the next several years between the abolitionists and their opponents, with John Quincy Adams leading the attack on the rule. He frequently engaged in shouting matches with the Speaker over what he called the flagrant violation of the constitutional rights of his constituents. Adams himself, however, violated House rules with abandon. "His whole effort being to produce irritation, throw the House into disorder," claimed one Democratic reporter, "and if he failed in everything else to waste the day in taking appeals from the decision of the Speaker on the rules of the House. . . . His object in making his numerous appeals was

41. *Congressional Globe*, 24th Cong., 2nd Sess., 1581ff.; Washington *Globe*, April 26, May 28, June 11, September 2, 1836.

not to obtain its sense but to waste its time." Democrats hooted their derision at him for his self-serving tactics. His only intent, they charged, was to even the score with Jackson on account of his defeat at the hands of democracy in the presidential election of 1828. This man, who had once told Congress not to be "palsied by the will of their constituents," was now taking his revenge by making a mockery of democratic procedures.[42]

To Andrew Jackson, John Quincy Adams was a hypocrite, pure and simple. His present behavior in Congress over the abolition petitions—as though Adams really cared about the slaves—only confirmed it. "Humanity and charity toward him, would say," Jackson declared, "that he must be demented, if not, then he is the most reckless and depraved man living." He was "reckless and depraved" because he deliberately endangered the integrity of the Union. The abolition question, wrote Martin Van Buren, was a vicious device "of evil disposed persons to disturb the harmony of our happy Union through its agency." To this, Jackson agreed wholeheartedly.[43]

The danger to the Union mounted when Texas won its independence and a movement began to engineer its admission. The abolitionists feared the spread of slavery into the Southwest and vigorously opposed annexation. Southerners, just as vigorously, warned that a failure to admit Texas could speed them out of the Union and into a new confederacy that would embrace the former Mexican colony.

Jackson involved himself deeply in the efforts to win ratification of a treaty of annexation after he stepped down as president.[44] What he wished to prevent was what he called an effort by Great Britain to form an "ascendency over Texas," for then "she would form a iron Hoop around the United States, with her West India Islands that would cost oceans of blood, and millions of money to Burst assunder." During the presidency of John Tyler the annexationists in the Senate planned to keep

42. *Register of Debates*, 24th Cong., 1st Sess., 2756–57; Washington *Globe*, January 28, February 4, 1837; Richardson (comp.), *Messages and Papers of the Presidents*, II, 882.
43. Andrew Jackson to Frank P. Blair, July 19, 1838, in Andrew Jackson Papers, Library of Congress; Martin Van Buren to Nathaniel Macon, February 13, 1836, in Nathaniel Macon Papers, Duke University Library, Durham, N.C.
44. His failures to win annexation while he was president are described in Remini, *Jackson and the Course of American Democracy*, 347–68.

the treaty a secret, once it was drawn up, until it was ready for submission to the Senate for ratification. "This prevents that arch fiend, J. Q. Adams," wrote Jackson, "from writing memorials and circulating them for signatures in the opposition to the annexation of Texas . . . to prevent the ratification of the Treaty, and giving time for all the abolition and eastern Federal papers, to fulminate against it [;] before this wretched old man can circulate his firebrands, and memorials against the ratifications of the treaty, it will be ratified by the Senate."[45]

Unfortunately, the treaty, signed on April 12, 1844, by representatives of the United States and Texas, went to the Senate accompanied by a letter written by President Tyler's secretary of state, John C. Calhoun, to the British minister in Washington, Richard Pakenham. In the letter Calhoun flatly stated that the treaty was intended to protect American slavery from British efforts to bring about universal emancipation. The action of the United States was meant to block that "reprehensible" effort.[46]

In reporting Calhoun's action to Jackson, Francis P. Blair claimed to know the nature of the South Carolinian's demonic scheme. And it was the same old contention—only now with a sharper focus. Calhoun intended to kill the treaty with his letter to Pakenham, the editor wrote, because it would "drive off every Northern man from reannexation" and provide him "a pretext to unite the whole South upon himself as the Champion of its cause." He was scheming to dissolve the Union, declared Blair, create a "Southern Confederacy" as the only means of winning Texas, and then "make himself the great man of this fragment which he expects to tear from the embrace of our glorious Govt." Shortly thereafter Blair wrote Jackson again and said, "It is quite clear now that Calhoun never meant that the Treaty should be ratified."[47]

Jackson agreed. He called Calhoun's letter weak and foolish and conceived simply "to arouse the Eastern states against the annexation of Texas. The power of the states over slavery," he added, "was not necessary by him then to have been brought

45. Jackson to Houston, March 15, 1844, from a private collection, copy in Jackson Papers Project, Hermitage.

46. Remini, *Jackson and the Course of American Democracy*, 496.

47. Blair to Jackson, May 2, 9, 1844, in Gist Blair Collection, Library of Congress.

into view." Why discuss this issue that had been settled by the Constitution—unless, of course, Calhoun intended all along to kill the treaty?[48]

It is hard not to agree with Jackson, Blair, and other Democrats about the mischievousness of Calhoun and Adams. For example, at one point Adams introduced into the House of Representatives a petition signed by forty-six Massachusetts citizens that Congress adopt measures to *dissolve the Union.* Adams asked that the document go to a select committee to draft a response explaining why the petition ought *not* be granted. Adams may have considered his motion a grand joke to make some dubious point about the freedom of petition, but in point of fact he deliberately raised tensions between sections that threatened to explode into something extremely serious. "Is Mr Adams demented," asked Jackson, "or is he perversely wicked. Both I think and Adams ought to be confined to a hospital."[49]

Adams may not have been demented, but he was deliberately mischievous. So, too, was Calhoun. Small wonder, then, that Jackson and his followers regarded them as "perversely wicked." For, as the *Globe* repeatedly warned, nullifiers and abolitionists were purposely exciting tensions between the sections with little thought about the danger to the Union. And the Jacksonians regarded both these groups as enemies of democracy, opponents of majority rule.

William Cooper in his book *Liberty and Slavery* has pointed out that an assault upon slavery was regarded by white southerners as an attack upon liberty.[50] But Jackson and his friends went further than that. They regarded an assault upon slavery as a calculated ploy to discredit the principle of majority rule and thereby bring the democracy into universal contempt, after which the wealthy few would regain their preeminence within the government.

Because it was deemed vital to let the American people know what General Jackson thought about the annexation of Texas, Democratic writers around the country published suitable quotations from his many public and private writings.

48. Jackson to Blair, May 11, 1844, in Jackson Papers, LC.
49. Jackson to William B. Lewis, February 27, 1842, in Jackson Papers, J. Pierpont Morgan Library, New York, N.Y.
50. Cooper, *Liberty and Slavery*, 179.

They especially liked one passage in which Jackson had said that the most compelling reason for annexation was "to give to this country the strength to resist foreign interference." For it cannot be doubted, he argued, that if Texas failed to gain admittance into "our confederacy," she would be driven into alliances with European powers of "a character highly injurious and probably hostile to this country." Thus, for Jackson and those who agreed with him, the desire for Texas had nothing to do with slavery and its extension. It had everything to do with national security. Jackson always insisted that annexation should not be a party question "but a national one." Once Texas was absorbed and "our laws extended over Orragon" and California, then "the perpetuation of our glorious Union" will be "as firm as the rocky mountains, and put to rest the vexing question of abolitionism, the dangerous rock to our Union, and put at defiance all combined Europe, if combined to invade us."[51]

The treaty of annexation was defeated, but ultimately Congress passed a joint resolution inviting Texas to join the Union. Unfortunately for Jackson, it did not put to rest the question of abolitionism, as he had hoped and predicted it would. The resolution was signed by President John Tyler on March 1, 1845, just three days before he left office. A few months later Jackson was dead, and the Jacksonian age virtually died with him.

But not abolitionism—even after Texas and Oregon and California were annexed. The bloody Civil War that ensued obliterated the "peculiar institution," but it also ushered in the age of the robber barons, just as Jackson and Blair had predicted.

The Jackson position regarding the slave question can be stated as follows: First of all, the Democratic party did not come into existence to serve as a bulwark of slavery. That was the mistaken presumption of John Quincy Adams—who needed to believe it after his humiliation in 1828—just as Calhoun's argument about the Tariff of Abominations was a mistaken presumption. (Between them, these two "perversely wicked" men have confused more historians over a longer period of time than any other two men in American history!) Nor was the Democratic party during its heyday under Jackson committed to the defense of slavery. Democrats believed that slavery was a fact of

51. Jackson to Blair, June 7, 25, 1844, Jackson Papers, LC.

life, that its existence in the several states was acknowledged and protected by the Constitution (like all other property), and that any tampering with it violated a compact among the states and endangered the balance that created the Union in the first place. What they did or did not do, therefore, reflected more than anything else their concern over what the nullifiers (Calhoun, Hammond, Waddy, Thompson, Pickens *et al.*) and the "Federals" (Adams, Slade, Granger *et al.*) would do in manipulating the slavery issue to achieve their own ends.

More important, Jacksonians convinced themselves that the slavery issue was really raised to impede the march of democracy. They could not help but view abolitionists as aristocrats who wanted to pull down the democracy that had displaced them. And the fact that the mobs producing the urban violence of the 1830s were led by "gentlemen of property and standing" in the community no doubt reinforced their perception.[52] Although Jackson did not have the empirical data provided by modern historians, he did know the leadership of at least one mob. After the Washington riot in August, 1835, a delegation of the leaders went to the White House to present their demands, and he spotted their pedigree and economic interests at once.[53]

Genuinely fearful for the future of the Union if abolitionists and nullifiers continued their violent actions, Jackson predicted civil war. And after that, he said, stockjobbing, land jobbing, and every other species of speculation would be carried into the legislatures, at both the state and the national levels, and produce an era of intense corruption in which the rich would plunder the nation and erect a government dedicated to their interests.[54]

The awful legacy of the Jacksonian age in failing to address

52. On this point see Leonard L. Richards, *"Gentlemen of Property and Standing": Anti-Abolition Mobs in Jacksonian America* (New York, 1970).

53. Washington *National Intelligencer*, August 12, 14, 1835; Washington *Globe*, August 19, 1835; "Narrative of Nicholas Trist," in James Parton, *Life of Andrew Jackson* (3 vols.; New York, 1861), III, 606–607; Remini, *Jackson and the Course of American Democracy*, 268–69. An excellent account of this phenomenon is Michael Feldberg, *The Turbulent Era: Riot and Disorder in Jacksonian America* (New York, 1980).

54. Jackson to Roger B. Taney, October 13, 1836, in Jackson Papers, LC; Jackson's speech in Columbia, Tennessee, quoted in Washington *Globe*, September 17, 1836.

properly the question of slavery as a moral question, a legacy that even Old Hickory himself gloomily predicted, was more a failure of omission than commission. This failure was not so much what the leaders of the Democratic party did in relation to slavery and abolition as it was their neglect of any opportunity to ameliorate the suffering of those held in bondage. They worried about the rights of white men; they hardly noticed blacks. They can be praised for their humanitarian concern for the plight of the poor—poor whites, that is. They deserve censure for ignoring the desperate needs of others.

But the legacy is not totally bleak. Although Jackson fulminated against those who endangered the Union and warned about the consequences of civil war, he remained basically optimistic about the future and the destiny of the American people. He believed the Union indestructible and certain to survive the paralyzing jolts administered by abolitionists and other malcontents. On the Friday before he died in 1845 Jackson spoke confidently of the future. "All is safe," he said. "There will be patriots enough in the land . . . to maintain sacredly our just rights and to perpetuate our glorious constitution and liberty, and to preserve our happy Union."[55] He also remained optimistic about the ability of the people to govern themselves and prevent permanent rule by a "corrupt money power." Not for a moment did he doubt the ultimate triumph of democracy. "I am delighted with the honorable rally of the democracy, the labouring classes, in the City of New-York," he wrote at one point. "They have done their *duty well*,—have given evidence of their virtue & patriotism, and that they will never surrender their liberty to the mony King or *bow the Knee to Ball* [Baal]. It has been a noble stand against the corrupt money power, and let the result be as it may, it affords ample proof that the peoples eyes are opening to the corruption of the times—the danger of their liberties from the mony power, and their determination to resist it. . . . Fear not, the people may be deluded for a moment, but cannot be corrupted."[56]

This Jeffersonian optimism about popular self-government and this romantic idealism about the incorruptibility of the people were matched by Jackson's unquenchable love of the

55. Parton, *Jackson*, III, 676.
56. Jackson to Van Buren, May 1, 1838, in Van Buren Papers, LC.

Union. For him these attitudes were his guideposts in approaching all questions, however simple, however weighty and complicated. They form part of the immense legacy Andrew Jackson left to future generations of Americans.

Not a bad legacy, that. It needs to be remembered.

Index